Robert MacLeod
Cowdenbeath Miner Poet

An Anthology by Arthur Nevay

Robert MacLeod

Cowdenbeath Miner Poet

An Anthology by
Arthur Nevay

Introduced and Edited by
Margaret Bennett

GRACE NOTE PUBLICATIONS

Robert MacLeod, Cowdenbeath Miner Poet
This edition is published by
Grace Note Publications in collaboration with
Arthur Nevay and Grace Notes Scotland, 2015

Grace Note Publications C.I.C.
Grange of Locherlour,
Ochtertyre, PH7 4JS,
Scotland

books@gracenotereading.co.uk
www.gracenotepublications.co.uk
www.gracenotescotland.org

ISBN 978-1-907676-73-4

Sponsored by Grace Notes Scotland as part of
'The End of the Shift' Project
Funded The Gannochy Trust and Grace Notes Scotland

Copyright © Robert MacLeod, 2015

Front Front: The Kirkford Pit, Cowdenbeath
and portrait of poet Robert MacLeod
Backcover: Photo of Arthur Nevay.

This book is part of an oral history project, 'The End of the Shift',
which records the memories, skills, and experiences of
former industrial workers in Fife and Perthshire.

This publication has been generously supported by

"Oh, God, protect and guide the miner,
Toiling for his daily bread,
Though his heart be light and cheery,
Dangers hover round his head."
Robet MacLeod

Contents

WAR

NATIONAL AND INTERNATIONAL EVENTS

LOVE AND AFFECTION

COMMUNITY, FAMILY AND NATION

FOOTBALL AND SPORT

Acknowledgements

"Bringing so many poems and songs together has been a delightful task and hopefully this publication will revive interest in MacLeod's work, as well as keep alive the social history, language and humour of a Fife mining community. May it also continue to bring pleasure and entertainment to future generations."

Arthur Nevay, Glencraig, 2015

This collection of Robert MacLeod's poems, songs and other creative work would have all but vanished were it not for the dedication and devotion of one person: Arthur Nevay, of Glencraig, Fife. We owe him a huge debt of gratitude, which, as far as 95-year-old Arthur is concerned, has already been repaid by the pleasure it brought to him, knowing that the name and work of Robert MacLeod will not be forgotten, and folk far and wide may enjoy his legacy.

We would like to thank all who have contributed to the many facets of this project: The MacLeod family, particularly his grandchildren Mrs. Aiken, Mr. A. Crawford, Mrs. Harvey, Mr. J. McLeod, Mr. T. McLeod, Mr. W. McLeod, Ms June MacLeod and her sister Irene; Mr. Jim Campbell (archive research); Mr. Bill Mitchell (photographer); The Benarty Heritage Preservation Group; Mr. Hugh Hoffman (Fife Family History Association); Mr. J. Stark (Central Fife Times); Mr. David Allan (Cowdenbeath F.C.); and Mrs. M. Gemmell (Adult Education Department, Fife Council).

As so many of MacLeod's poems and songs light up the social history of his time, they are an important part of a much wider heritage. We would like to thank the Heritage Lottery Fund and the Gannochy Trust for supporting the Grace Notes Scotland project, 'The End of the Shift', which preserves industrial heritage. This book is the third and last book of the project, and it has been a real mile-stone to see it in print. Through this grant, every library and school in Fife will have a copy of Robert MacLeod's work.

Thanks also go to Michelle Melville, Jennifer Meiklejohn and Ann Petrie who transcribed the recorded interviews and manuscripts; to fellow poets who lent an ear and gave advice: William Hershaw, Tom Hubbard, Adam McNaughton, and Joy Hendry; to singer Scott Gardiner ('Bothy Scott'); to music-hall advisors Stuart A. Harris-Logan (Archivist) and Andy Dougan (Film & Television Studies) at the Royal Conservatoire of Scotland, and Judith Bowers at the Britannia Panopticon in Glasgow; to Gonzalo Mazzei, who designed the cover and typeset the book; and to Ros and Russell Salton for proof-reading several versions of texts. (Any errors that may have crept back in are the responsibility of the editor, who would appreciate updates for any future edition.)

Finally, we would like to thank Fife's own Barbara Dickson for her enthusiasm and encouragement. In her own life of song, Barbara has been one of Scotland's finest ambassadors in the world of entertainment, and she shares our hope that MacLeod's songs will have a new lease of life as young singers add to their repertoire and sing them the world over.

To all who have shown interest, lent a hand, or an ear, and given support of any kind, our sincere thanks.

Margaret Bennett, Editor
Grace Notes Scotland, 2015

Introduction

In tracking down or piecing together local histories, academics may be more inclined to head for the library or archives than the hairdresser's salon or the music-hall. If the research of 95-year-old Arthur Nevay is anything to go by, however, those interested in Scotland's mining areas will welcome a wealth of social history that may have been over-looked. Arthur, who had a career in hairdressing, has lived in the Fife village of Glencraig since his family moved there when he was only six months old. In those days, Glencraig was a thriving mining community, and one of Arthur's earliest memories is of the police presence during the 1926 Miners' Strike:

> We lived in Gary Park, and the Police had a march through the street with batons – huge batons over their shoulders, like troops, and it was really a frightening experience for a child of five years of age. I think I've always been a bit sensitive, and it quite obviously that impressed me.

As with this recollection, countless others were to become imprinted in Arthur's memory. His father, James Nevay, trained as a barber in Dundee, then managed several salons before opening his own business in Glencraig. Most of his customers were miners, and, as more than 1,300 men worked in the pit, Jimmy Nevay had a successful business until the 1926 strike. Work ground to a halt, as did wages and livelihoods, and the aftermath was to last a long time, as Arthur recalls:

> In the Twenties and the Thirties I've seen so much poverty among the miners. During the Depression, there was a large unemployment period, and in fact my father lost his business through the 1926

Strike, because he had no money to pay his rates. But he paid every penny back to the people he was due money to, and it took him from 1926 until 1939 to pay that money back, though legally he didn't require to do so. During the late Twenties and the Thirties I'd seen the effects of the strike. Like, for instance, you had, a lot of men were unemployed, and Thursday was the busiest day we had in the salon because that was the day that the unemployed got their ten shillings a week. They walked from Lochore, Crosshill and Glencraig to Lochgelly on the Tuesday to sign on – they had no money, but they went to collect their few shillings on the Thursday, and if they had a copper or two left to get a haircut, well they got a haircut. *[Can you remember what the usual cost of a haircut was, when the strike was over?]* I can remember quite well. For a man it cost fourpence, and for a boy, thruppence, and the shave was thruppence, and it went up from four-pence to six-pence for a man and four-pence for a boy.

Despite the hardships of those hungry years, Jimmy Nevay gradually built up the business, and Arthur followed his father's footsteps: "My father used to tell me, 'He who listens, learns.'" It is often said that if you are looking for a good listener, or a sympathetic ear, make an appointment with your hairdresser. Arthur not only listened, but, the age of 95, he recalls 'who was who' in the village when he was a boy, citing where they lived, who their relatives were, who were school classmates, who they married, and where they found employment. Arthur's eyes light up with memories, and he has an endless repertoire of anecdotes that include conversations and witty remarks:

> The one-time manager of Glencraig Colliery, Andrew Crow, used to say there's more coal

stripped in Jimmy Nevay's Barber shop than there is at Glencraig Colliery! Stripped, by the way, means produced, and this was him emphasising that they probably weren't working as hard as they should have been. But of course he was one of my best clients for the simple reason that, when the haircut was about a shilling, I used to get half a crown from him. At that time he was the General Manager for The Wilson and Clyde Coal Company, and he used to come to visit Glencraig Colliery, back and forward, and he always come in for his haircut then.

Though 'coal was king' for most of Arthur's life, he explained that that had only been the situation since his father's time, as the Glencraig pit was sunk in 1897, and within a few years hundreds of families moved. "In 1891 Glencraig was composed of five farms, a row of three farm cottages, a shepherd's cottage, and Glencraig House." Arthur has been collecting information about the history of the area for years, and in 2013 was named Citizen of the Year, in honour of his life-long contribution to local histories. Having amassed decades of photos of Glencraig, as well as manuscripts, maps, letters, and newspaper cuttings, he compiled a comprehensive book about the village. He even did the printing and binding, then, with the help of a technical expert, set up his award-winning website, 'The Lost Village of Glencraig'.

Being a member of the Benarty Heritage Preservation Group, which meets weekly, Arthur has enjoyed the benefits of being surrounded by enthusiasts who share his commitment. As there may be few areas of Scotland that have undergone so many changes in landscape and life-style as Fife, there is a sense of urgency to record every aspect of life in the mining communities. Together and individually, members have worked on projects that have amassed information about the lives of miners and their families, the work they did, the hazards and accidents, the clothes they wore, their contribution to two world wars, and so on. Carefully they collect and archive every detail, from the distant past to the recent experiences of the pit closures, contributing to a website with a vast array of photos and information that would otherwise have been lost. In pulling together skills as well as information, members of the group encourage each other, sharing expertise and ideas, as they continue to add to their invaluable archive and online resources.

One of the great strengths of belonging to such a group is that it keeps the mind active and tuned in to the heart of the community and its history. When Arthur was asked how he acquired such an encyclopaedic range of local knowledge, he was typically modest, attributing all of it to the people who surrounded him in his day to day work. From the time he began his career, Arthur regarded his busy hairdressing salon as the ideal arena for discussions:

> I always found that the miners were great debaters and some of their debates and arguments with each other were away beyond what you would expect from a man going down into the bowels of the earth to cut coal. It's always amazed me...

Perhaps more amazing is that Arthur recalls minute details that he heard eight decades ago. He is always on the alert for interesting information that may turn up when least expected, such as when he first came across the writing of a miner from the nearby village of Cowdenbeath, Robert MacLeod:

> In the late Eighties, there was two of MacLeod's grandsons, William and Thomas MacLeod, who did my garden, and they were bringing tatty pieces of paper that you could hardly read, things about their grandfather, and I said to them eventually, "Ach," I says, "Collect all these bits of paper you have lying about, and bring them down to me." So

I think they brought about twenty grubby pieces of paper down to me, and I then got in touch with the local newspaper and asked if anybody had MacLeod poems.

Arthur's letter in the *Fife Times and Advertiser* caught the attention of readers, and among the respondents was Fife song-maker John Watt (1933–2011), whose own songs are known the world over. (He may be best known for 'The Kelty Clippie' and 'Pittenweem Jo', and, in football circles, the name of John Thompson of Bowhill, Cardenden is immortalised by Watt's song about the young goal-keeper.) Alas it is too late to ask John for more information, but, from the personal tone of his letter (referring to the poet as 'Bob' rather than 'Robert'), he seems to have known MacLeod:

> Some marvellous writings have stemmed from Bob's pen. As most of Bob's poems exist in either small booklet or broadsheet form, what a marvellous opportunity this presents. Many people in the Lochgelly and Cowdenbeath area must still be in possession of these works. Is there some interested person, or educational body willing to collate this mass of important material and produce a book? If enough broadsheets are still in existence, they would not have to be reset. They could be used as camera-ready copy and reproduced in their original state. Lines like "Away ye big brushers[1] frae Lumphinnnans and the Peeweep" should not be forgotten!

Praise from a song-maker of Watt's stature is praise indeed. This, and other letters, elicited a response from MacLeod's daughter, the late Mrs Elizabeth MacArthur, who lived in Dunfermline:

---

[1] The brushers are the men in the colliery who do the dangerous work of removing part of the roof or pavement (by blasting or other means) in order to heighten the roadway for the miners. So far, we have not come across the poem quoted by John Watt.

Many thanks … for the warm tributes paid to my father, Bob MacLeod, in the "Times". The fact that my father can be written about in this way – 31 years after his death – filled me with pride, as memories came flooding back of the 1926 Strike and the soup kitchens, back-green concerts, "Go as you Please" competitions and Parish Relief. No strike or holiday pay then.

Bob MacLeod thought he was just a cog in the wheel of mining communities who gave their all, but he was an inspiration to all who knew him because he suffered much. I often wondered, as I saw him perform on the stage, at the courage and spirit of the man who had survived two mining accidents, which broke his hip, his thigh, his knee, tore off his heel and ankle and left him with only five toes. It was the long stays in hospital and painful operations that ended his career as a singer. [Yet, out of adversity] the "Miner Poet" was born, whose one ambition was to make people laugh, although other people's worries and accidents affected him deeply.

The "War Effort" was an example: when Craven A and Kensitas sent him boxes of cigarettes that were sent out to the troops in the Middle East. It was a proud moment when Field Marshall Montgomery wrote thanking the people back home for the "fags", which were a great morale booster.[2]

Mr. John Watt asked if there is some interested person or educational body willing to collate my father's mass of material and produce a book. I echo these sentiments entirely but, being ignorant

---

[2] Over the years, MacLeod's daughter Elizabeth combined information from several letters. See Appendix.

of how to go about it, I would welcome any advice.

Arthur clipped out the letters and added them to his collection. Each bit of paper was saved like vital pieces in a huge jig-saw puzzle that had no picture on the box: "I gathered over a hundred poems, but sad to say not the tunes."

Although some of the broadsheets (mentioned by Watt) turned up, as well as two little chapbooks, most of MacLeod's compositions have been hand-written, copied and re-copied by folk who enjoyed them and wanted to pass them on. While this may be frustrating for the researcher who is looking for an original, it is also a great compliment to the poet, for it is only 'maakers' with real appeal whose 'screivin' is circulated in this way. It is all part of the living tradition, and, apart from rote memory, has been by far the most common way that songs travel from singer to singer, or place to place.

Having collected this omnium-gatherum of papers, Arthur typed them out, page by page, and in so doing, became conversant with the entire corpus of poetry and song:

MacLeod was a very unusual man, regarding his poems, the way he covers such a range of topics. Like, there's one about his wee sweetheart when he was five years of age, 'Bonnie Wee Nell o Spinkie Dell', set in a wooded glade:

I loved a wee lass as dear as my life,
Oft times we promised tae become man and wife,
But she vanished from memory, sad story I'll tell –
Often she gathered the wild flowers around Spinkie Dell.

To me, he captures the innocence of young love… Besides this kind of delicate poem, he has so much social history in his writing. For instance, he has a poem about the Titanic; he has one about Scott's expedition to the South Pole; he has two about flights from America to Britain: one successful and one unsuccessful. In reading his poems and songs, I've given Robert MacLeod a lot of thought – in my mind, a man that could write this sort of stuff … [he's quite complex], for instance, on one hand he's a great Royalist – I mean, he sent copies of his poems to Buckingham Palace, which were acknowledged – and at the same time he was a great Trade Unionist. Regarding his personal life: he was working in the mine, but really his ambition was to be a song and dance man, on the stage. There was the Tivoli, which was a theatre in Cowdenbeath, and he used to appear there, along with some of the great Scottish names in his day – he performed alongside them. It would appear from some of the comments that I've heard indirectly about MacLeod, he was good, and these people all had a great name for him.

With the passing of time, today (2015) there are very few people who met Robert MacLeod or heard him sing. Among them is his grand-daughter, June MacLeod, who lives in Dunfermline. She has bright, childhood memories of visiting her beloved 'Grandi', though until she read the articles in the *Fife Times and Advertiser*, (1989), she had no idea that he was a poet or song-maker. June got in touch with Elizabeth ('Aunt Lizzy') and meeting Arthur was a real highlight for both of them, especially as he gave them biographic information neither had heard before:

> Robert Johnston MacLeod was born in Musselburgh in 1876. His father Sinclair MacLeod hailed from Prestonpans and his mother Elizabeth from Tranent, where five of their children were born: Sinclair (1862), Elizabeth (1864), Annie (1869), Maggie (1872), and Thomas (1875). The family then moved to Musselburgh, Robert's birthplace, before

moving to Markinch in Fife, where their youngest
son, Archibald, was born (1879). In 1887 they moved
to Cowdenbeath, which became home to Robert for
the rest of his life.

In Robert's youth, the school-leaving age was twelve[3], with an
option to stay on, though most families relied on their children
to seek work as soon as possible. For the boys, it went without
saying that they would go down the pit, like their fathers
before them. Though there is no exact record of when Robert
left school, there can be no question that he was well educated.
His writing shows a high standard of literacy, and his poems
and songs reflect a wide knowledge of literature, world history
and current affairs. Destined to become a miner, however,
Robert was employed by Kirkford Colliery in Cowdenbeath. To
thousands of miners, however, the end of school did not mean
the end of education, but a transition to what is now called 'life-
long learning'. All over Fife folk tell of the importance of the
local libraries, as well as the much-frequented reading rooms,
which enabled generations of miners to become the well-
informed citizens they became.[4]

Until the age of 25, Robert lived in the family home at 6
Foulford Road, and helped support his mother, who had been
widowed. On the 4th June 1901 Robert married Janet Crawford,
a local pithead lass, who lived at 75 Union Street. The wedding
was at the Registry Office in Chambers Street, Edinburgh,
attended by two of their friends, Janet's neighbour, Isabella
Watson, and fellow-miner Robert Davidson from Cardenden.
The couple made their home in Cowdenbeath, where they were
to raise their family of five sons and three daughters.

Hard work, long hours, dark, unhealthy and dangerous
conditions were a way of life to the miners, while their wives

---

[3] It was not until the Education Act of 1918 that the school leaving age was
raised to 14 and local authority fees were abolished.

[4] For example, in the mid-1800s, Kirkcaldy had five libraries, including a Me-
chanics' Library, which was one of the first in Britain.

took on an unspeakably arduous role. As Arthur's friend and local community Councillor Willie Clarke put it, "The miners were slaves, but their wives were slaves of slaves." Yet, to this day, most families remark on the close-knit communities that lifted their spirits.

Once a year the mining villages held a gala, which brought the entire community together. Even today, when there are no coal-mines, Fife has several Miners' Gala Days, which are always well planned in advance. As Arthur remarked, everyone looked forward to turning out in their Sunday best to enjoy every moment, for it was one of the few days when folk were free from dust, damp, darkness and danger:

> The miners contributed a penny a week to the children's gala day, and when the gala come along all the prizes for the different races and competitions that they held, for Highland dancing, running and that, culminating in the marathon, which was the main event. That was the last event and that prize was a suit of clothes. And the winner of that, oh, was a king! I mean he was good at running for one thing, and he was appreciated for that, but the enviable fact was that he was getting a suit of clothes to take home!

Robert fitted in to the miner's lifestyle, though his dream was to be a music-hall entertainer. Elizabeth remembered his fine tenor voice, and how he loved to sing, dance and to make people laugh until the horrific injuries sustained in Kirkford Colliery almost cost him his life. A beam gave way and fell on him, Elizabeth explained, as she reflected on how the accident affected the whole family, for her father lost his livelihood as well as his hope of making a career as an entertainer:

> It was to take nearly a year in hospital before he would know if his broken leg could be saved. His hip and his thigh were broken and part of his foot

was severed, when the toe of his boot was ripped off – he lost some of his toes, and when he eventually got home he had to wear a special boot. It was his long stay in hospital, watching and hearing the nurses going about their duties, that the comic and 'Miner Poet' was born.[5]

MacLeod's considerable output of poetry suggests that, like Burns, he had been jotting down lines of verse from an early age. The poem to which Elizabeth refers is called 'Takkin a Rest', which he wrote when the nurses were preparing for Christmas. Robert was among the patients who would not be able to go home so, making the best of things, he joined in the spirit of the occasion:

> And we're gaun tae hae a concert,
> That's my chance to mak a hit;
> I'll sing them the "Camlachie Scout",
> As in my bed I sit.

Written in his hospital bed, Robert's title is full of irony, for well he knew the miner's longing for rest from the relentless twelve-hour shifts. This kind of rest, however, was every miner's nightmare.

In his mid-thirties, Robert's working life was over. As far as can be gathered, there is no record of the date of his accident, though, according to the 1911 Census, he was still working as a miner – Robert was 35 years old, Janet was 33 and they lived at 137 Foulford Road, Cowdenbeath with their four children: John, age 9 (b. 1902), Robert, age 7 (b. 1904), Thomas, age 3 (b. 1908), and Jeannie, age 3 months (b. 1910). The couple had also known the sadness of losing a child. That same year may also have been when Robert's accident occurred, as the following year, on October 1912, Robert signed his name on a new poem, and wrote his address as 79 Union Street, Cowdenbeath. We

[5] Quotations from the poet's daughter Elizabeth are from a a one-page essay written at June MacLeod's request and used with permission.

can only guess whether the move from Foulford Road was by choice, or because they could no longer occupy a house owned by Kirkford Colliery, or because the access was no longer suitable, given the injuries Robert sustained.

By 1914, the start of the Great War, Robert could no longer earn his living as a miner, nor could he 'answer the call of King and country', to take part in a war that was to devastate so many families, including his own.[6] Yet his poetry shows how deeply he felt the losses of so many, and how closely he followed every news-report, both local and international.

Elizabeth, who was born in 1913, was too young to remember her father's efforts to support the troops. Though she was only five years old when the war ended, she often heard about how he sold his poems to raise money for the war effort. Despite having to support his family without a wage, he gave the proceeds from his war poems and songs to buy 'comforts' for the troops. The poems and songs speak for themselves, and his generosity and compassion are also reflected in the correspondence he received during the Second World War. Among the papers that Arthur collected are thankyou letters from the War Office, from Field Marshall Montgomery ('Monty'), from two cigarette companies, and even from Buckingham Palace. (See Appendix)

Janet and Robert MacLeod had three more children, Janet (b. 1916), David (b. 1918), and Archibald (b. 1925). Though others might have murmured "one more mouth to feed," this is not what we hear in Robert's poem, 'The Smile of a Child':

> *In her little cot where she goes to sleep,*
> *While angels, silent, watch over her keep,*
> *When in dreamland where she loves to be,*
> *The smile of a child is heaven to me.*

Although the children over twelve worked to earn their keep, nevertheless it was a daily challenge to provide for the family on a poet's earnings. During and after the 1926 Miners' Strike,

---

[6] Robert's brother was killed. See his poem 'My Brother'.

poverty was rife, and MacLeod's grand-daughters June and Irene recall their Dad (David) telling them of one time when they had no money and the only food in the house was a cabbage. Their grandmother cooked it, but "there was no butter or anything to put on it so he used tally grease from the oil lamps to flavour it."[7]

Although children of June and Irene's generation grew up with post-war rationing, the austerity of the Fifties seemed like luxury compared to what their father experienced during the Twenties. Scarcely able to imagine how hard it must have been, the girls wanted to hear more:

> We'd all be round the kitchen table and we'd ask our Dad to tell us stories about when he was young. He said they were so poor that they went to school barefoot in summer and they only wore shoes in winter. It was hand-me-downs, whatever shoes fitted you, and they often had holes in them. They rarely had a pair of shoes that didn't have holes in them, and they wore really tatty clothes, and one time he went to school he had thirteen patches on his trousers, and he was so ashamed. But he got to school and was in his class, and his teacher called him up in front of the class and he thought, "Oh, no, I'm in trouble for all these patches on my trousers," and the teacher stood him in front of the class and she said to the children, "Now I want you all to look at David's patches on his trousers and look at how well they're stitched. They're beautifully stitched!" She praised the patches so much that Dad went home that day feeling so proud!

No mining community will forget the time when every family felt the effects of the strike and the depression that was to

---

[7] Before the introduction of the carbide lamp, the miners' lamps were fuelled by tallow grease, which was animal fat, usually from sheep, cattle or pigs.

last more than a decade. Standing in the House of Commons in 1957, Fife miner Tom Hubbard (b. 1898), who eventually became MP for Kirkcaldy, took the opportunity to tell his fellow-parliamentarians what it was like:

> In 1926, in common with all miners, I was locked out. My employers refused to continue my employment on the conditions that had been negotiated between miners and mine owners. I was disqualified, along with everybody else, from drawing unemployment benefit. Having a wife and two children, I qualified for public assistance.
>
> We were compelled to live on 11s. a week. That would have been bad enough had it been paid in cash, but the amount was given in the form of a voucher. It gave us the experience of concessions, tokens and coupons. When my wife went out to buy groceries, the grocer had to go to other shops and purchase her meat and bread for her. We got no change from those vouchers, which had to be spent in one shop. We could not go from one shop to another to purchase what we wanted. That horrible experience we had for seven months.[8]

Soup kitchens became a feature of every mining community, and Robert MacLeod's daughter Elizabeth recalled that her father did his best to raise money to help the starving miners and their families. When the community organized fund-raising events, she remembered that "he wrote his own material then dressed as a woman to hide his crippled leg, and was always a star turn at concerts organised to raise money for soup kitchens and other worthy causes." He loved to make people laugh, and in the hey-day of the music-hall, the audiences flocked to enjoy the entertainment which lifted everyone's spirits. Robert

---

[8] Tom Hubbard later became Labour MP for Kirkcaldy. This was part of a speech he made in Parliament, November 19, 1957. (Quoted from Hansard.) In decimal currency, 11 shillings is 55 pence.

had a good singing voice and played the accordion, and, as his poetry and songs show, he could be hilariously funny, witty, mischievous and playfully irreverent, with 'one-liners' that could not fail to raise a laugh. Nevertheless, the audience would never have suspected the effort and sheer grit it took just to dress to leave the house. Elizabeth, who used to help her father get ready for a show, had vivid memories of what it was like: "Only those nearest to him knew the pain he suffered in trying to perform the simple task of washing and drying his feet and then trying to tie his boot laces – two things he could never do for himself." For his audience, however, Robert had to look the part on stage, dressing in "a tartan waistcoat and bonnet. He wore the yellow tartan, the MacLeod of Lewis dress tartan, and his boots were very highly polished."

Though MacLeod may have had no connection to the Isle of Lewis, his choice of tartan was probably based on his keen sense of stage presence and performance – the 'yellow MacLeod' stands out and makes an impact. A Skye connection seems more likely as he published his poem, 'Skye' in the local paper, *The Clarion of Skye* (1953). That being so, his people would have been Gaelic-speakers, and though there is no mention of the language, some his poetry echoes of the internal rhymes and assonance (underlined below), characteristic of traditional Gaelic poetry:

> The promise was _fine_, I longed for the _time_
> When the dinner hour bell it wad toll,
> My bunnet I'd _grup_, then hame for a _sup_
> Oot my mither's auld fashioned blue bowl.[9]

Photographs of Robert wearing his feathered bonnet are reminiscent of many of the music-hall entertainers of his day, particularly Harry Lauder, who had become world-famous. Robert MacLeod composed several of his songs to Lauder's tunes, sharing his sense of fun in parodies such as 'Bella in the

---

[9] From his poem, 'My Mither's Auld Fashioned Blue Bowl'. Though lines 2 and 4 have end-rhymes, the internal sounds seem stronger.

Bath', to the tune of 'Will Ye Stop Yer Tickling, Jock'.

Though the gramophone had become popular by the turn of the twentieth century, acquiring one was a huge consideration for working-class families. Nevertheless, the wind-up gramophone became a major source of community entertainment, for when a family in better circumstances managed to buy one, their house became a gathering place for neighbours. Eventually, however, the MacLeod family got their own wind-up gramophone, which June and Irene remember from their childhood:

> It was like a black box, you lifted the lid to put on the record – it was the old 78s that broke very easily. My Dad had a great big box of old 78 records and it was in the family for years and years. They'd been in Grandi's house then in ours – 'Granny's Hieland Hame', I remember that one. [10] There were old fashioned Scottish songs … Harry Lauder too. You'd wind it up, and sometimes you'd be half way through a record and then it would go, waaaaaaaaaah! [as it slowed down] so you'd to wind like mad to keep it going! I remember the needles, those tiny little needles in a wee tin, and when they wore down we used to sharpen them because we couldn't buy replacements.

Busking became a way of life for Robert, and over the years he turned out a steady stream of poems and songs. Many were inspired by local and national events as well as the social comment of the day. He had an eye for local characters and could also poke fun at situations or incidents, giving folk something to laugh about instead of giving in to gloom. June and Irene had often heard their father tell them: "Grandi would go round as many pubs and clubs as possible, singing and dancing to

---

[10] The song is attributed to Sandy MacFarlane (Alexander MacFarlane), who was born in Scotland and emigrated to America as a young man. He recorded the song on 78 rpm disk Columbia DB152.

make money to keep his family, and for his cigarettes and a wee dram, though I'm sure he had plenty bought for him." As carrying an instrument from one location to the next would have been almost impossible for him, "Uncle Rab and Uncle Tom would go with him and carry the accordion, the button-box, and they'd go round with the hats while he played and sang. He also went to any concerts that were offering prizes."

Though he lived with daily pain and disability, MacLeod believed in living life to the full. No longer able to kick a football with his mates, far less work with them, he still shared their passion for the game and especially for the local team. It is in this area that Robert MacLeod is best remembered, having penned over twenty compositions celebrating and supporting 'Cowden'. In the early days, the Cowdenbeath team was often called 'The Miners', though is now better known as The Blue Brazil. The club's historian (as well as Finance Director), David Allen, who also edits the magazine and Blue Brazil programme, remembered Robert MacLeod's support for the team. When he read Arthur's letter in the *Fife Times* (1989) he joined the discussion and wrote to the paper:

> His connection with Cowdenbeath F.C. was as a supporter but, more importantly, as a chronicler in rhyme of events at Central Park for over 40 years... In his lifetime he wrote several hundred poems, many of which were published in the local press. In the 1920s, there were poems re Cowden heroes such as "Willie Devlin on the baa" and "Willie Pullar wi the twinkling feet" which he would sing to the tune of "Barney Google" while the 1950s brought poems such as "Keep Cowden at the Tap" and "Cowden's Daein' Fine" as Cowden went for promotion in 1957... A recent book on Rangers was illustrated with a photo of a card featuring a poem by Robert MacLeod on Rangers' great winger Sandy Archibald (from Crossgates) – "Sandy, ye're

a Dandy". He also was a singer and entertainer in the 1920's during the Miners' Strikes. His last poem was on the subject of the Lindsey Pit Disaster [1957]. When he died the following year at the age of 82, Cowdenbeath lost one of its personalities and Cowdenbeath F.C. lost a great supporter when the man they called "the Miners' Poet" died.

Referring to Robert MacLeod as 'the Miners' Poet' (occasionally 'the Miner's Poet'), became common, even among MacLeod's family, though it was not the term that Robert himself used. His printed poems and broadsheets have his own appellation, 'Robert MacLeod, Miner Poet'. While his choice may reflect his sense of fun (if not pun) as well as his modesty, it also affirms his keen awareness of the subtleties of grammar, spelling and language usage. Reading his work, there can be no doubt that MacLeod was totally conversant with Scotland's major poets, but, equally, he was content to take his place among the minor poets. His aim was to light up days that were otherwise dark and dreary, and his poetry and songs reflect his positive, optimistic and thankful attitude to life. Robert MacLeod chose to ignore the fact that fate had dealt him some severe blows, and instead he focused on the very best of life's gifts, to be shared with family and friends.

Looking back to childhood memories of her grandfather, June MacLeod reflected, "He was a lovely man, soft spoken ... He had a good head of white hair ... But I didn't even know he had a limp! I didn't notice and nobody mentioned it." Her grandfather was 72 years old when June was born, so he no longer needed to busk as he had qualified for the Old Age Pension at the age of 70. He and Janet had moved to 99 Thistle Street, where, in the closing years of their lives they enjoyed basic comforts denied in youth.

Irene also remembered Granny and Grandi visited their house in a nearby street: "It was to our prefab at 4 Meadowfield in Cowdenbeath. Granny dressed in a long black skirt and boots and she always wore her grey-white hair tied back in a bun. She was a lovely lady and very well spoken but looked very frail." The sisters were amused and surprised when their Dad told them that "Granny used to smoke a clay pipe and she used to go about with this white clay pipe in her mouth, even when it wasn't lit."

June and Irene were very young when their grandmother died (November 17, 1952), and after her death, most of the visits were to the house on Thistle Street. June remembers going to visit Grandi with her father, and still pictures him welcoming them at the door:

> Oh, it was great! It wasn't in a miners' row, but it was so dark inside – it was a dark, dingy house; everything seemed to be brown, and dark colours. And straight ahead, as you went through the door, there was a big, wooden sideboard, cupboards at the sides and drawers down the middle, and he would open the top drawer and take out a thruppenny bit, which we used to get from him. And there were recesses in the wall, to the left, two big recesses, and this was the bed recesses, cos it was a one-bedroom house. Uncle Arch stayed with Grandi – he was the youngest and he never married and continued to live there for many years after Grandi died. There was a family Bible and the birth dates and any deaths of the children were written inside the front cover. Grandi was very religious … and Dad could recite verses from the Bible so they must have gone to church… Probably Church of Scotland, but I'm not sure which one.

The name of the exact church seems irrelevant to June's memories of a family and community that had a rootedness and strength she no longer senses. Her fellow-citizen, the Rev. Ron Ferguson also looks back to a time when Cowdenbeath churches were filled with miners and their families. Writing about a way of life that they once took for granted, he speaks (or writes) for many mining families:

> It was a gritty, compassionate community which closed ranks when adversity struck – and it struck often... The stability of that community life stands out now. My father lived in Cowdenbeath all his days... worked all his life... was married to the same woman ... lived in the same council house ... survived two World Wars ... He attended the same kirk, at a time when the sight of working men at public worship was not something to be marveled at...[11] I remember with pride how the churches in Cowdenbeath stood by the miners in their time of trial... I was drawn to faith by the quality of the lives of the members ... I knew instinctively they were people I could trust.

Coal dust was part of life, and so also was cigarette smoke. As many folk remark, "Everybody smoked... some folk used to say it was good for you... but that was before they knew about the effects on health..." Robert MacLeod was no exception, and June recounted her father's memory that "he often tried to stop and would get angry and throw his boots across the room. He cut down to one at bedtime." Too late, however, to have escaped illness, complicated by an intestinal tumour that was to prove fatal:

> Before he died he was taken to a country hospital in Dundee in the hope that getting away from a mining village and getting some good country air would help him. Sadly, he didn't make it and died of lung cancer on the 9th May, 1958, although it wasn't a known illness in these days.[12]

---

[11] Ron Ferguson, *Black Diamonds and the Blue Brazil*, p. xxxv followed by p. 175.

[12] According to his death certificate, the cause of death was Malignant Neoplasm of bowel, (exact site unknown).

In reflecting on her childhood memories, June regretted the fact that she never heard her grandfather sing:

> I didn't even know until after we heard about Arthur's collection, then I found out more from Arthur than from my own Dad. It was later in life before I heard that he was a miners' poet – I found out after he died. Have you heard anything about 'Ye Cannae Shove Yer Granny aff the Bus'? My Dad told me when I was young that Grandi wrote 'Ye Cannae Shove Yer Granny aff the Bus'. Now when I was going to school, it was a school bus, and the children would be singing the song on the bus, and I would say, "My Grandi wrote that," and they would just laugh at me, they'd say, "Oh, your Granda never wrote that!" But he did, he wrote it, and seemingly he couldn't afford to get it [copyrighted]. And I hear it sung on television, coming home on the bus everywhere – but I just think, "Oh I'm not going to mention it; nobody'll believe me." I kept a few of his papers, and he always wrote in pencil.

Encouraged by Arthur, June began to search through her father's papers, where she found several pieces, yellowed with age. Several were printed by a Cowdenbeath printer, some were in Robert's own hand-writing, a few were carbon copies of typed pages and others were spirit-copied:

> Everything he had seemed to be on this brownish paper or bright blue-green paper. Some of these were in a little booklet, and I copied them out. I sat hour after hour and typed them out and put them in a folder to add to Arthur's collection and I made four copies for my family. I made clean copies of all of them, but I didn't keep the old ones in brownish paper… But if I'd actually known, I'd have kept the originals.

Among the assortment of papers in Arthur's collection was a letter, hand-written in 1912, when he was still recovering from his accident and coming to terms with the fact that the injuries would probably shorten his life. Making light of the grim prospects, it is addressed to the local grave-digger. The lay-out is an example of letter-writing as it was once taught in every Scottish classroom, though the reader soon gets the sense that this is a poem from the poet who had spent over a year in hospital.

79 Union Street,
Cowdenbeath,
Fifeshire.

26th. October 1912.

To the Grave Digger
Jimmie Wiseman
Kirk o Beath.

If I die and loss my braith, jist tak me up tae Kirk o Beath, and hand me ower tae Jimmy Wiseman, He'll only think he's got a prize, man.

When he sees the hearse comin ower the ben, He'll cry, "Wha is this ye hae the day?"
The driver he'll say, "Dinnae speak aloud, It's only oor poet, pair Robbie MacLeod. So open yer gates and let us through, And his last request we'll tell tae you.
Noo Jimmy, lay him cannily doon, for ye ken he wis a funny loon. He wrought beside yer wee son Johnnie, wha wis Robbie's faithful cronie. He made the best o his spare oors, and brocht Robbie mony a bunch o flouers,[13] but noo pair Mac has slipped awaa, and Johnnie has nae pal ava.

---

[13] This verse suggests that Robert's friend and work-mate brought flowers when he visited the hospital,

The last words that Bobbie said, "Tell Jimmy tae be canny wi the spade, and when he's got me in a corner, let him play at Johnnie Horner."

Noo Jimmy Wiseman, try yer best, and gie puir Robbie his last request."

Robert MacLeod,
Miner Poet

He was to live for another 46 years, thankful for each one, and determined to use his time and talents making the miners' world a brighter place. Having spent all his life in a mining community, Arthur Nevay knows that world well, for he has lived through almost a century of the ups and downs that brought out the best in Robert MacLeod. In bringing together this collection Arthur shows the same generous spirit that allows us all to share MacLeod's legacy.

Margaret Bennett,
Hon. Prof. of Antiquities and Folklore, RSA, Edinburgh.
Hon. Lecturer and Research Fellow, University of St. Andrews.

The MacLeod family welcome home David, on wartime leave from the Middle East, 1943.

Robert MacLeod

Foreword

Twenty-first Century Reflections on Cowdenbeath's Pitman Poet

Pick up the local paper, traditionally referred to in households as "The Two Minutes' Silence", and there is a good chance that a citizen will have felt the need to put pen to paper or digit to keyboard to give expression in a form of verse. Some contribute regularly and build up a local following over time. As with all forms of poetic utterance the quality of the verse can vary, but the precedent and role of the local poet is still well understood even in today's world. While sales of tabloid and 'quality' newspapers have fallen in the online age, The Tuppenny Rag holds its ground still. Perhaps, in some places where traditional forms of day-to-day communal interaction have been eroded or even broken down, the function of the local paper is even more important: whatever areas it covers, the Letters Page acts as a conduit, allowing folk to express what concerns them and also, over a period of time, functions as an archive and annal of the parish. If Robert MacLeod were to return today he might have initial difficulty embracing the complexities of the social media but he would surely recognise this continuing tradition.

The collected body of MacLeod's poems and songs is nothing less than an extended time capsule of his lifespan that provides a comprehensive and fascinating insight into life in a Fife mining community during the first half of the twentieth century. In a recent radio ballad recorded for the BBC, the Northumbrian songwriter Jez Lowe sings "These things I know, for the Pitmen Poets told me so …" This line sums up exactly the role of poets such as Robert MacLeod: to record in verse the everyday happenings, concerns, attitudes, relationships, thoughts, feelings, celebrations, songs and tragedies of the local mining folk.

In the following pages the reader will find little that describes the practicalities of coal mining itself, i.e., what was physically involved in bringing the coal up to the surface. Perhaps it was thought too well understood to waste words on; perhaps it was too unpleasant to dwell on. Apart from the poems commemorating the significant pit disasters (all of them similar in style and sombre diction) there is not much about the actual job of the miner. Instead, what we have in abundance are the individual and communal collected joys, sorrows and humours of life in a mining community - an all-embracing theme that is inclusive of women, bairns and menfolk. That is why, regardless of how he signed himself, Robert MacLeod justifies the epithet of a "Miners' Poet": a sense of shared values is what defined mining communities as much as the back-breaking labour and the filthy, dangerous conditions.

Unlike a mining poet such as Joe Corrie, there is no overt political stance, endorsement of party or attempt to persuade readers to alter their view in MacLeod's work. There is a stoical acceptance of the harsh realities of life from time immemorial: the miners are badly paid and treated; the mine owners cannot be trusted to play fair in their greed for profits; the union is a necessary bulwark against this; in time of need or war the government will come running to the miners for help but in the meantime it cares little about unemployment and poverty. In a nutshell: life is a hard struggle and always will be. In MacLeod's work there is no sense that it was ever any different or that it will ever change. It was inconceivable that the reign of King Coal might end in MacLeod's time. In this unchanging universe difficult conditions of life are to be faced up to in the same way as the flu epidemic or the continual struggle to find enough money for food and rent.

Throughout it all, however, there is an optimism that the spirit of the mining folk will overcome and prevail. There is a sense of joy and fun that runs through his work. Likewise a strong sense of patriotic unionism that goes hand-in-hand with intense local pride. In MacLeod's world it is possible to be a proud British subject and an equally proud and independent Scotsman. The union is accepted as one between equal partners. The poet feels entitled to put pen to paper to mourn the loss of a member of the Royal Family because he views it as his role to express a shared grief. Even the elegy to a brother killed in the Great War makes no complaint or questions the sacrifice.

An accident down the pit nearly ended MacLeod's life at an early stage and also deprived him of the opportunity to escape the pits through a career on stage: yet the showman in him is evident in the poems and songs: the sense of drama, the pawky and satirical humour and the love of occasion. It is in his songs that he comes closest to what might be defined as 'the folk tradition'. While acknowledging the continued importance of the letters page we might ask, "Why poetry?" The answer is that the power and effect of rhythm and rhyme on the human consciousness, going back to preliterate times, has never diminished. Encasing descriptions of events in rhyme and rhythm makes them not only memorable but provokes emotion in the reader. MacLeod uses the Scots language and local dialect to make us laugh and to create pathos and bathos. He uses a more formal serious "English" tone to record tragedy. He knows what he is doing and uses words deliberately to create the desired effect. He is not T. S. Eliot, though. His verse is literal, with little reliance on traditional "art" poetic imagery such as metaphor or simile. He represents a link between the folk balladeers of the eighteenth and nineteenth industrial centuries and the changed technological post-Great War world that brought radio, television and much else into the lives of working people.

> Robert MacLeod is the commentator of parish events but he also translates events and news of the outside world into the language of the parish.

Many of his songs are set to popular tunes from the music hall (Stop Yer Ticklin Jock) or folk tunes (Johnny Scobie, Loch Lomond). At this remove it is difficult for us to fully appreciate the enormous popularity of entertainers of the day such as Harry Lauder. By setting his words to weel-kent tunes, MacLeod would have ensured oral transmission as well as through the pages of the paper. Folk from Cowdenbeath, Kelty and Lochgelly would have picked up on the cleverness of the parody and the satirical digs and references. MacLeod was their bard, their 'Pitman Poet' and stands proudly among others such as James R Murray or Auchterderran's John Pindar (Peter Leslie - The Soldier Poet) and of course, the great Joe Corrie, who rose up to the light of international fame from the Bowhill pits. Arthur Nevay's collection provides a fascinating record of a Scotland that has all but vanished, but also celebrates the lively intelligence, humour and spirit of a unique Scotsman of his time.

William Hershaw
Poet, writer, and teacher at Beith High School, Cowdenbeath
Lochgelly, 2015

Poems

Pits and Politics

A Collier Tae A Flae

Ye little black troublesome cratur,
By jings ye're an awfu raker,
The moment I think o gaun tae bed,
'Tis there ye're wanting tae be fed.

I screw doon the lamp, I look the time,
And then prepare for the pantomime,
But when I try tae faa asleep,
Ower my weary limbs ye start tae creep.

I find ye nippin at my puir shanks,
Ye're up tae aa kind o pranks,
Wi me ye're kickin up the deuce,
But no sae bad as yer freen the louse.

Ye're loupin, flingin, jinkin, prancin,
An ower the blankets ye gang dancin,
I'll hae tae rise and get the poker,
And be after ye, my little joker.

Ye little ken whit ye are daein,
Ye little ken whit is abrewin,
For this it cannae dae wi me,
I rise at five, it's gaun tae three.

I get the poker ower the bed,
And on the pillow I lay my head,
And there I lie and wait my chance,
Waiting on the enemy tae advance.

I fling doon the claes tae hae a look,
Only tae find ye've slung your hook,
In tae some corner warm and snug,
Perhaps beside yer freen the bug.

The clean sheets Jenny did rub,
Aa day lang at the washing tub,
Ye've made them like a draught-board noo.
Nae wonder that I'm in a stew.

Ye little, dirty, ill-bred scamp,
On my puir airm ye've left yer stamp,
Wi a wee red dotty in the centre,
Which proves yersel tae be a penter.

But I'll catch ye yet, my little nipper,
And wi you I'll play "Jack the Ripper",
If I get ye, my pey I'll gamble,
I'll put ye through the blooming mangle.

I try again tae faa a-snorin.
When at my legs I find you borin.
And when I rise tae hae a keek,
As efter ye I start tae seek.

I see ye poppin oot yer nose,
Wonderin whit's wrang, I suppose,
Sittin on a braw clean blanket,
I think it's time ye should shank it.

I spit on ma fingers, I then tak aim,
For I've been often at the game,
As I'm a sinner, again I've missed ye,
The devil tak ye, I never blessed ye.

And noo the clock has chappit fower.
Time that I was drappin ower,
But for a nicht's fun ye are bent,
Ye'll think yersel ye pay the rent.

For want o sleep my een turn sair,
I fling the bed claes on the flair,
And noo I wish I had a byke,
Tae chase ye up and doon, ye tyke.

But there's the wife crying, "Rab, it's five,"
I moan oot mair deid than alive,
"Jenny I cannae work the day,
As I've had a sad night wi a flae".

A Collier to A Flae.

By

ROBERT McLEOD,

Miner Poet.

Ye little black troublesome craitor,
By j ngs yer an aefu' raker,
The moment I think o' gaun tae bed,
'Tis there ye'r waitin' to be fed.

I screw doon the lamp, I look the time
And then prepare for the pantomime.
But when I try to fa' asleep,
Ower my weary limbs ye start to creep.

I find ye nippin' at my puir shanks,
Ye'r up tae a' kind o' pranks,
Wi' me ye'r kickin' up the duce,
But no sae bad as ye'r freen the loose.

Ye'r loupin', flingin', jinkin' prancin',
As ower the blankets ye gang dancin'.
I'll hae tae rise and get the poker
And be efter ye my little joker.

Ye little ken whit ye are dain',
Ye little ken whit is abrewin',
For this it canna dae wi' me,
I rise at five, it's guan tae three.

I get the poker ower the bed
And on the pillow I lay my head,
And there I lie and wait my chance,
Waitin' on the enemy to advance.

I fling doon the claes to hae a look
Only to find ye've slung yer hook,
Intae some corner warm and snug,
Perhaps beside yer freen the bug.

The clean sheets Jenny she did rub,
A' day lang at the washing tub,
Ye've made them like a draught-board noo,
Nae wonder that I'm in a stew.

Ye little, dirty, ill-bred scamp,
On my puir airm ye've left ye'r stamp,
Wi' a wee red dotty in the centre,
Which proves yersel' to be a penter.

But I'll catch ye yet my little nipper,
And wi' you I'll play "Jack the Ripper,"
If I get ye, my pey I'll gamble
I'll put ye thro' the bloomin' mangle.

I try again to fa' a-snorin'
When at my legs I find ye borin',
And when I rise to hae a keek,
As efter ye I start tae seek.

I see ye poppin' oot yer nose,
Wonderin' what's wrang I suppose,
Sittin' on a braw clean blanket,
I think its time ye should shank it.

I spit on my fingers, I then tak' aim,
For I've been often at the game,
As I'm a sinner, again I've missed ye,
The deevil tak' ye I never blessed ye.

And noo the clock has chappit four,
Time that I was drappin' ower,
But for a nicht's fun ye are bent,
Ye'll think yersel' ye pey the rent.

For want o' sleep my een turn sair,
I fling the bed claes on the flair,
And noo I wish I had a byke
To chase ye up and doon the tyke.

But there's the wife cryin', "Rab, it's five,"
I moan oot mair deid than alive,
"Jenny, I canna work the day,
As I've had a sad night wi' a flae."

My Man's On The Buroo

My man's on the Buroo, my man's on the Buroo,
A gey sad time for a puir woman the noo;
Frae morning tae nicht we're aye on a battle,
Whit he brings tae me widnae buy wee Jean a rattle.

He's awaa at nine o'clock staunin oot in the cauld.
I'm vexed for him noo, he turnin gey bauld;
His jaws they are clappit, his nose it is blue,
I'm sorry tae tell ye my man's on the Buroo.

For dinner I used tae hae a guid pot o kail,
But noo I've tae dip a bane in the pail;
When the bairns come hame their noses they screw,
Aa ower their daddy being on the Buroo.

I dinnae ken what I'm gaun tae dae,
The baker is greetin, the grocer's tae pay;
The press it is empty that aince was gey fou,
But that hisnae happened since Jock went on the Buroo.

The ither day oor packman come up the stair
And demanded money frae me, I declare;
Wi the wee kitchen poker I struck him on the broo,
And printed these words, "My man's on the Buroo."

Mind Jock's a guid worker if he gets the chance,
A braw fechter tae, he did that in France;
And this is whit he's getting efter aw he's come through,
A sad day for me if he ends on the Buroo.

But I'll get my neebour, big Leebie Broon,
And whaur they pay oot, we're baith gaun doon;
And mind I tell ye there'll be a hullabaloo
If oor men's no gaun tae get mair aff the Buroo.

The Glencraig Pit Disaster, 21st May 1918

In which Birrell Davidson Junior lost his life; Cameron
and Hay being saved by the bravery of Inspector James
Simpson.

Deep down in the depths below,
Three miners entombed lay,
They were daring, hardy sons of toil:
Davidson, Cameron and Hay.

'Twas at the deadly hour of night,
There came a sudden crash,
And Davidson was pinned to die,
Beneath that treacherous mass.

Brave Inspector James Simpson,
Did all that was in his power,
To try and save his fellow-man,
In that awful trying hour.

He worked, my God, but not in vain,
And cleared the redd away,
By doing so he saved the lives,
Of young Cameron and Hay.

May God protect the miner,
When down at his adverse work,
While toiling for his crust of bread,
Where dangers ever lurk.

O comfort those who are left to mourn,
And their burden bravely bear,
May they gather in that home above,
Where all is happy, bright and fair.

The Main Link o The Chain

Hats off tae the miners every one,
They're worthy o the name,
Frae the pulley wheels tae coal face,
He's the main link o the chain.

Frae early in the morning,
He toddles tae his wark,
He leaves the glorious sunshine,
And the merry singing lark.

Doon in the depths he struggles on,
His bread there tae maintain,
And yet he never stops tae think,
He's the main link o the chain.

Ye lords wha sit there at yer ease,
In aa yer grandeur fine,
Ye never think on the trials he has,
When toiling in the gloomy mine.

But if the link should snap,
The country's doomed again,
And then Coal Jock is sadly missed,
The main link o the chain.

'Tis then they want the wee bit coal,
And there's neither spark nor flame,
Tae warm the taes on wintry days,
Wi the missing link o the chain.

The sailor ploughs the angry deeps,
The sodger toes the line,
But still they have a hardy chum,
The miner doon the mine.

But when death gies the fatal blow,
There lies his worn out frame,
When gane tae rest may he be blessed,
He's the main link o the chain.

The Miner Tae The Midge

Wee harmless craiter wi glossy wings,
Ye mak oor lips utter oot sic things,
Us collier chaps flee in a passion,
When shovels and picks begin a-clashin,
At yokin time the jackets come aff,
We licht oor pipes and start tae chaff,
The tiny visitor comes on the scene,
And looks for a restin place gey clean.

But still we ken ye'll dae nae hairm,
As ye go creepin up oor airm,
Ye keep us on the move I'm shair,
Hoo ye bother us little dae ye care,
Ye hae us gey often in a fidge,
Although ye're only a wee pit midge,
Some rough chiel will hit a crack,
Takkin a stick tae break his ain back.

The moment ye see the blow a-coming,
Roond his lugs ye're fairly bumming,
Ye're ticklin noo, he cannae check,
As ye move careless ower his neck,
'Tis then on him ye're playin a prank,
And tae his work he has tae shank,
Shovin his hutch but little thinkin
That after him ye will be jinkin.

He cannae hear yer wee wing flappin,
As at a length o rails he's chappin,
Then doon on him ye mak a dive,
Tae let him ken ye're still alive,

His neck again he's sairly spankin.
While for a braith o air he's pantin,
And on his heid his lampie's burning,
Clawin his airms and oh the murnin!

Then taks the lamp doon in his hand,
Expectin the midge on it tae land,
Or waitin tae gie ye a wee bit lickin,
Or catch ye on the lamp nose stickin.
But ye're very cute, the licht ye'll shy,
Wishin on piece time drawin nigh.
When that time comes we club the gither,
As ye go fleein hither and thither.

Ye'll better watch the cunning spider,
Working hard on his tiny fibre,
Ye will be numbered wi the dead,
If ye land upon that fatal web.
Ye little buzzer, ye're aye on the mooch,
What impudence gaun intae a collier's pooch!
But the thing that puts us in a hoax,
Hoo the devil ye get in oor piece box?

We tak aff the lid and there ye're sittin,
Ye wad mak folk think ye were first fitten.
Takkin maist onything ye please,
Worryin intae the breid and cheese,
But whiles ye put yersel in a puzzle,
As oor butter an jam ye start ta guzzle,
Wi oor lamp picker we try tae free ye,
Juist a while langer o life's pleasures tae gie ye.

Wee silly craiter whit makes ye sae greedy,
Frae a simple miner sae puir and needy?
On him for yer mite ye hae depended,
And yer short life ye noo hae ended.
Yer motionless body noo at rest,
Yince wi the collier ye did jest,
Tae lose yer company oh! hoo we grudge,
Tae pairt wi oor freend, the wee pit midge.

The Redding Pit Disaster

Near Falkirk, 25 September 1923.

'Twas at the break of the dawn,
When our heroes went down below,
Never dreaming of their danger,
When there came a dreadful blow,

A sudden burst of water,
All round our heroes true.
Struggling for life they clung together,
My God, what more could they do?

A cry of distress and they were flocking,
News of the flood a gloom had spread,
But the worst was yet tae come,
The task of bringing up the dead.

Sorrowing mothers and weeping children,
Waiting on loved ones tae claim,
Looking anxious for dear faces,
In life they may never see again,

While in homes sad hearts are beating,
Oh! what grief they now have felt!
Little ones in sadness praying,
Beside their mother's knee they knelt.

Mamma, tell, where is daddy?
Why is he not coming home?
With his fond and warm kisses,
Has he left us all alone?

Oh your dad, my child, she whispered,
As she wiped away a tear,
He has died with his comrades
Down the mine so dark and drear.

Men in garb and grime of toil,
And willing hands they did not lack,
But their attempts were all in vain,
With black damp they were driven back.

Tears filled the eyes of those assembled,
A chill of horror passed through the crowd,
While lips of strong men quivered,
As they wrapped their mates in shroud.

Deeds of the rescuers will be remembered,
They were heroes every one,
Not a moment did they hesitate,
While there was duty tae be done.

Oh, God, protect and guide the miner,
While toiling for his crust of bread,
Though his heart be light and cheery,
Danger hovers round his head.

Fathers, mothers, sisters, brothers,
Sweethearts, children and dear wives,
Pray that heaven may reward them,
Those hardy sons who lost their lives.[1]

---

[1] When no words seemed to express the deep sadness felt by the loss of loved ones, MacLeod, like the traditional ballad-maker, resorted to stock phrases and oft-repeated expressions. Being as close to the situation as he was, it is not surprising that he echoed his own lines when trying to come to terms with yet another awful disaster.

The Union Man[2]

Written in 1925

In me ye see a Union man,
These five and twenty years;
Tho' I hae been hard pressed at times,
I've been seldom in arrears.
Ye ken that unity is strength,
So if ye tak my plan,
Juist be like yer humble freend,
And become a Union man.

When ye are boilin doon the mine,
And gettin shair an shair alike,
Aye be fair wi yer fellow-man,
Wha's strugglin for his bite.
The books are open tae ye noo,
It disnae pey tae scan,
But hurry an jine, ye'll be in time
Tae become a Union man.

When trouble knocks upon the door,
And things are lookin glum,
It very often visits the poor,
And in it shairly comes,
So this advice I gie tae you,
And dae the best ye can,
Tae yersel juist say, "I'll go this day
And be a Union man."

---

[2] Though he signed and dated his poems, only a few of the original papers
survive, and most of the copies are text only, without the date.

The Valleyfield Colliery Disaster

28th October 1939, 35 precious souls went to their doom.

'Twas on a cold October morn
Our miners were down below,
Never thinking of the danger
When came the dreadful blow.

A bad explosion had taken place
All round our heroes true,
Side by side they bravely perished,
My God, what more could they do?

Cries of distress and crowds were flocking,
News of the fire a gloom had spread;
And the worst was yet to come,
The task of bringing up the dead.

Sorrowing mothers and weeping children
Waiting on loved ones to claim,
Looking anxious for kind faces,
In life they'll never see again.

While in homes sad hearts are beating,
Oh, what grief they now all felt!
Little ones in sadness praying,
Beside their mother's knee they knelt.

"Mamma, tell me where is my daddy,
Why is he not coming home?
With his fond and warm kisses,
Has he left us all alone?"

"Oh, your dad, my child," she whispered,
As she wiped away a tear,
"He has died with his comrades
Down the mine so dark and drear."

Men in garb and grime of toil,
Strong, willing hands they did not lack
But their attempts were all in vain,
With foul air they were driven back.

Tears filled the eyes of those assembled,
A chill of horror passed through the crowd,
While the lips of brave men quivered
As they wrapped their mates in shrouds.

Deeds of rescuers will be remembered,
They were heroes every one;
Not a moment they hesitated
While there was duty to be done.

Oh, God, protect and guide the miner
While toiling for his crust of bread;
Although his heart is light and cheery,
Danger hovers round his head.

Fathers, mothers, sisters, brothers,
Sweethearts, children and dear wives,
Pray that heaven may reward them –
Those hardy sons who lost their lives.

The Lindsay Pit Disaster

Kelty, 14 December 1957.[3]

Deep, deep down in the dreary mine,
When Death's dark angel came,
And tore from them their loved ones,
In life they'll never see again.

Oh! Cruel was that dreadful blow,
That struck with all its power.
And left sad hearts to grieve,
In that fatal morning hour!

Down among the deadly fire,
Far away from God's fresh air,
Perished our true hardy sons,
Who were once our tender care.

Willing hands were there and ready.
To do their duty every one,
But alas, their task had ended,
The deadly gas its work had done.

And our hero, brave David Scott,
Into the fiery furnace ran,
And gave his life most dearly,
To try tae save his fellow man.

---

[3] This was Robert MacLeod's last poem, as he died the following year. The sense of loss and profound grief still affects the community, where each December the people of Kelty gather to remember the miners who lost their lives, as well as the families whose lives were shattered by loss. The emotion affects everyone, bringing people together, of all faiths and none, in the oft-repeated prayer, 'Oh, God, protect and guide the miner, toiling for his daily bread...'

Fond hearts in grief were waiting,
Their dear loved ones to enfold,
But now all hopes were vanished,
As rescuers their sad story told.

Oh, God, protect and guide the miner,
Toiling for his daily bread,
Though his heart be light and cheery,
Dangers hover round his head.

Bless those in sad homes weeping,
For the dear they did love,
Pray that Heaven will reward them,
In that eternal home above.

Community and Family

A Day Wi the Bairns

I saw the bairns on parade,
And shouted oot, "Hooray!"
And every ane was overjoyed
For it was their Gala Day.

The mothers had a busy time
Turning them oot sae braw,
And telling Jean and Meg
Tae watch and dinna faa.

Hundreds lined the thoroughfare
As the bands began tae play,
And sic a crood o bonnie bairns
On their happy Gala Day.

Wi flags and banners waving high
Tae the park they marched away,
They got a treat o things sae sweet,
Aa on their Gala Day.

And when the racing it did start,
Hoo oor Johnny he did rin,
While aa the rest gaed tumblin
Ower a slippy banana skin.

There's Isa, Liz and Jenny
They're nearly aa wan size,
They're knockin ane anither ower
Tae try and get a prize.

At last their little feet got sair,
As each one duin their best,
Wi racin here and racin there
They were ready for a rest.

And when the sun was sinkin low,
Hameward they went their way,
And aye they'll thank the weather clerk
For a glorious Gala Day.

COWDENBEATH CHILDRENS GALA, 1950
Approaching Kelty Junction from Perth Road

Guid Auld Santa Claus

There is a time o year comes roond,
When oor bairnies yin an aa,
Wonderin just what they will get
Frae the guid auld Santa Claus.

He comes when they are sleepin,
When there's neither haa nor hum,
At twelve o'clock wi his big poke
He draps canny doon the lum.

He creeps up tae each little bed
And their stockings he does fill,
Then he pats them on the heid
While they are sleepin still.

They waken in the mornin
Withoot the slightest fear,
And cry oot tae their mither
"Has Santa Claus been here?"

They ken fou weel he wid come
Wi drums and bugles braw;
They look for somethin every time
Frae guid auld Santa Claus.

There's a coach tae little Annie
And a pug tae little Tam
And a motor car tae Johnnie,
And tae Jean a wee pet lamb.

Noo Santa he kens whit tae bring
He never plays the fule
Tae aa the guid boys and girls
That gaun every day tae schule.

Sae dinna forget auld Santa,
Tae you he will be dear,
He wishes you a merry Christmas
And a happy New Year!

Harry Hope's Fish Shop

At the corner of Union Street.

There's a Fish Shop in oor toon,
It looks sae trig and braw,
For cleanliness and civility,
Ye get that when ye caa.

The fish they sell is o the best,
Ye'll say they're up-tae-date
And aye ready tae serve ye,
Come early or come late.

So when ye visit Cowdenbeath
And hae a while tae stop,
Caa in and tak a guid fry hame,
Oot o Harry Hope's Fish Shop.

John McEwan's Choir

Last Sunday I visited the P.S.A.
It was my heart's desire,
Tae listen to the pieces sung
By John McEwan's Choir.

They opened with their "March Along",
And oh, but it was fine,
Conducted by John himself,
Wha kept them well in time.

The solos sung were o the best,
They filled oor herts wi glee;
The trio it was blended weel
In songs o Victory.

And every ane gied o their best,
They aa kept weel in time,
Oh! whit a treat, where we did meet,
On the Sunday afternoon.

The people there aa clapped their hands,
They enjoyed it ane and aa;
A smile it beamed on every face
Before they gaed awaa.

Noo, if ever I get sad at heart,
And a tonic I require,
Tae the P.S.A., I'll go straight aff
And hear John McEwan's Choir.

My Mother

Who nursed me at her loving breast,
And did her all to give me rest,
Who should I love the very best?
     My Mother.

Who rocked me in my cradle bed,
And gently stroked my little head?
And oh! the kindly words she said,
     My Mother.

Who taught me to say my evening prayer,
And knelt beside me at my chair,
And told me of the angels fair?
     My Mother.

Who watched over me in my sleep,
Till the dawn began to peep,
Through the night her watch did keep?
     My Mother.

Who forbade me to tell a lie,
Told me true that God was nigh,
And of the heavenly home on high?
     My Mother.

Who will I love when growing old,
When her trembling hands turn cold?
Oh! may she wear a crown of gold!
     My Mother

MY MOTHER.

Who nursed me at her loving breast,
And did her all to give me rest?
Who should I love the very best?
     My Mother.

Who rocked me in my cradle bed,
And gently stroked my little head?
And oh! the kindly words she said,
     My Mother.

Who taught me to say my evening prayer,
And knelt beside me at my chair,
And told me of the angels fair?
     My Mother.

Who watched o're me in my sleep
Till the dawn began to peep,
Through the night her watch did keep?
     My Mother.

Who forbade me to tell a lie,
Told me true that God was nigh,
And of the heavenly home on high?
     My Mother.

Who will I love when growing old,
When her trembling hands turn cold,
Oh! may she wear a crown of gold.
     My Mother.

                R. McL.

My Mither's Auld-Fashioned Blue Bowl

When I wis a laddie and went tae the schule,
My mither whiles at me did scowl,
Noo mind and no fail and you'll get your kail
Oot yer mither's auld-fashioned blue bowl.

The promise was fine, I longed for the time
When the dinner hour bell it wad toll,
My bunnet I'd grup, then hame for a sup
Oot my mither's auld-fashioned blue bowl.

"Stand up Jamie Dunn, ye're wrang wi the sum!"
The Maister wi the tawse made me howl,
Wi the tear in my ee there wis nae kail for me
Oot my mither's auld-fashioned blue bowl.

But I put the coont richt, ran hame aa my micht,
Like a cat through the hoose I did prowl,
'Twas there on the stove, the feed I did love,
Oot my mither's auld-fashioned blue bowl.

I then got a spune, supped it tim frae the rim,
Then I dichted my chin wi a towel,
My mither I'd bless for I couldnae miss
That favourite auld-fashioned blue bowl.

And it's my dearest wish tae treasure this dish,
It belanged tae a decent auld soul,
Noo it stands on the shelf 'mang the rest o the Delft,
My mither's auld-fashioned blue bowl.

Takkin A Rest

I oft thocht I could tak a rest
But I'm getting ane at last:
It's four weeks noo since I come in here,
And I wish this rest was past.

I dinnae get a wink at nicht,
For folks crying through their sleep:
They yell for pans and bottles,
But I cry oot for meat.

The nurses hae a busy time
Running wi the barraes
They serve a lot o them in here,
It wud tak a dizzen lorries.

I dinna eat very much masel,
I could be daein wi mair;
Ye wud hardly see me in the bed,
If it wisnae for my hair.

I hear there's gaun tae be a feast,
It happens on Christmas Day
So I'm takkin every nicht
Tae be ready for the fray.

And we're gaun tae hae a concert,
That's my chance to mak a hit;
I'll sing them the "Camlachie Scout",
As in my bed I sit.

The only thing that I'll no get,
Is a drink o Bass's Beer,
But I'll juist hae tae be a Templar,
Till efter the New Year.

At least they've asked me for tae sing,
But I doubt I'll no be able,
The smell o the turkey'll cut ma breath,
And I'll faa below the table.

I'm expectin tae get oot then,
But my feet they will be tender,
So ye'll hae tae gae up tae the smith
And order a little fender.[4]

The doctor says I'll need it much,
For my leg is a little shorter;
I tellt him it was short before,
He said, " Mac, you're a corker!"

So freends, aa dear, ye'll think I'm queer,
But I hae duin ma best;
I've juist noo got my paarich,
So I'm gaun tae hae a rest.

---

[4] Orthopaedic patients had to make their own arrangements for orthotic devices, such as leg-braces, because there were no facilities in hospitals until after the Second World War. As leg-braces were made of iron, they could be made to specification by the local blacksmith – the 'smith' in this poem.

The Auld-Fashioned Dish (Caaed 'the Po')

There's an auld-fashioned dish an it's every-yin's wish,
We search for it high and low,
A freen I may say, baith nicht and day,
The auld-fashioned dish caaed 'the Po'.

For morning exercise it comes as a prize,
When physic it makes ye cry "Oh!"
Ye sit at yer ease as lang as ye please,
On this auld-fashioned dish caaed 'the Po'.

Wi a paper at hand, oh, man it is grand!
Ye look the columns high and low,
If yer team's won the day, tae cry oot hoo-ray!
On this auld-fashioned dish caaed 'the Po'.

At a wedding or spree where'er ye may be,
When freens meet and feel cheery oh;
When the morning is busy, Mary and Lizzie,
Will slink ben the room to 'the Po'.

Noo auld Granny Green kept hers gey clean,
And a bonnie design that is so,
It was flouer'd roon the side, aince her ain mither's pride,
This auld-fashioned dish caaed 'the Po'.

Wi a big rosy fire, that's aa ye require,
Ye feel quite at hame, dae ye no?
Heated weel roon the rim, then ye'll kick up a din,
On this auld-fashioned dish caaed 'the Po'.

When a couple get wed, they slip intae bed,
It has been duin lang, lang years ago,
But it's a race, dae ye see, wha's to get the first 'pee',
In this auld-fashioned dish caaed 'the Po'.

The Auld Toll Hoose

The Auld Toll Hoose has stood for years,
In the burgh o Cowdenbeath,
But at last it has been aa torn doon,
And it comes tae us like a daith.

It suffered mony a heavy blast,
O cauld winter's sleet and snaw,
And has sheltered mony an auld collier,
That's lang syne deid and awaa.

And even in the summer time,
Some thocht it wis a treat,
Tae sit behind its wee thick waas
And shun the burning heat.

And when a laddie at the schule,
I've played the truant there,
And dodged the whupper-in, it's true,
And took it as a tear.

And weel I mind on the Jubilee Day,
We sat upon the tiles,
And got oor photographs aa taen,
Wi aa oor funny smiles.

It was kept by Jamie Murray,
For sixteen years I'm shair,
A weel-kent barber in the toon,
Wha fairly could shave and cut hair.

He liked tae sit among the auld hands,
Tae hae a guid nicht's crack,
And pass a wee bit joke at times,
For at them he wisnae slack.

So we bid a fond fareweel tae the Auld Toll Hoose,
The hoose we loued sae dear,
We may regret but canna forget,
We'll miss ye, year by year.

The Auld Toll House, Cowdenbeath, was demolished in 1907.

The Awfu Flu

The Flu, the Flu, this awfu Flu,
It's visited me, has it visited you?
It grips ye sae sudden, it gies ye nae chance,
They say it comes frae Spain or France.[5]

It comes floating ower here amang oor ain folk,
It tickles yer throat till ye're near fit tae choke,
Yer heid it sets bummin, it maks ye look blue,
This awfu epidemic, they caa it the Flu.

Our doctors are runnin aboot wi their cars,
They're awaa frae the wan place tae some ither ane
waur,
And women are cryin, "Doctor, come juist the noo,
For the hale o my household are laid doon wi the Flu!"

They're using up pencils writing oot lines,
I can speak for masel and they bairns o mine's,
Frae morn tae nicht I'm aa in a stew,
It's gien me some work this terrible Flu.

Even daiths are takkin place wi this awfu stuff,
If ye're twaa days in bed ye're fair oot o puff,
At aa druggist shops it's raisin a queue,
Wi this horrible trouble they caa the Flu,

---

[5] The flu epidemic of 1918 is still regarded as the worst the world has ever
known. The death toll was estimated to be twice that of World War 1.

The men coming in, the kail-pat's no on,
A gey braw like thing tae look upon,
A bed fu o bairns, a gey pityfu case,
I cannae get time tae wash my face.

It's gey high time it wis fleein awaa,
If it wad what a blessin it wad be tae us aa,
For my pairt this mineet I could bid it adieu,
As I've haen ma ain shair o this awfu Flu.

The Carsebrig Craws

The Carsebrig Craws, they sit in raws
When days are getting dusky:
They cannae steer, they feel sae queer
Wi the fumes o' Carsebrig Whusky.

Up in the trees they sit and sneeze,
Alang the branches they dae patter:
Ye'd ken the smell had taen their heids
Wi their cletter and their clatter.

The distillery there juist under-neath,
Gey weel they ken the place:
Tae get the best position
Ye wad think it wis a race.

They're flockin here and flockin there,
And kicking up a funk:
In less than a trice, they think it nice,
Tae see ane anither drunk.

So if ye want a guid craw pie
Awaa and get yer gun,
And hae a pop at the drunken crew –
Ye will enjoy the fun.

I'll go, I'll go, and face the foe
As shair's my name's McClusky,
And chase the craws that sit in raws
And smell the Carsebrig Whusky.

The Gift o The Gab, (Or A Mither's Advice)

Written in 1925.

Like mony ither body I was born gey young,
And my mither she christened me Rab,
She said, "Ye'll get on in life, dear bairn,
If ye just hae the gift o the gab."

And oh! Hoo she kissed me and caressed me,
And caaed me her innocent bab,
She'd hush me tae sleep, and these words wad repeat,
"If ye only hae the gift o the gab."

When I began tae toddle I started tae gabble,
At my playmates I had mony a dab,
My mither wad cry, "Robbie, dinnae mak that yer hobby
– But aye hae the gift o the gab,"

I went tae the schule tae be made a scholar or fule,
Said the maister, "Ye're as thick as a slab,"
Wi the tawse he wad thrash me, oot the door clash me,
Wi my little bit gift o the gab.

As I grew older, I aye grew bolder,
And intae mischief I would lab,
But my puir mither kept crying in my ear,
"Will ye juist hae the gift o the gab?"

"Aye, try to be honest," my mither wad say,
"Dinnae rob the puir collier or snab,
But be like a man, look the world in the face,
 And aye hae the gift o the gab."

The Handy Wee Man In The Bar

There's a handy wee man in the Beath Tavern,
And the customers frae near and far,
They find it delight tae get a bit light
Frae the handy wee man in the bar.

He stands there alane, oot his mooth shoots a flame,
And he ne'er says a word aboot war,
Sae obliging is he tae baith you and me,
This handy wee man in the bar.

So when ye gang in juist slip ower tae him
Wi yer pipe, cigarette, or cigar;
He stands there at ease and you he will please,
The handy wee man in the bar.

He ne'er asks a drink, sae what dae ye think,
Wi his pen and handsome ink jar,
It's really worthwhile tae get a nice smile
Frae the handy wee man in the bar.

When we gang that way for a bricht holiday,
Wi the tram, bus or braw motor car,
He's there tae greet you and proud tae meet you,
The wee man in Willie Archibald's bar.

The Sink

Weel hoo are ye, Mrs Johnstone?
I'm feelin fine masel.
Gosh! Ye're asking me a question
That I dinnae care tae tell,
I'm feelin that awfu worrit
Wi ma man aye takkin drink,
For every nicht when he comes hame
He peedles in the sink!
Fal-de-dal

He gangs tae Masons' meetins,
Whit he daes I cannae tell,
It seems they canna mak me yin;
I've nae place tae hing the bell.
And then he'll sing "Walk in the Licht,"
And at me gie a wink
Then stagger richt across the flair,
And peedles in the sink.
Fal-de-dal.

Noo when the meetin's ended,
And they're wendin their way hame,
Some gang alang the back road,
And some by "Courtin Lane"
And they aa pee agin the waa,
But my man, the waur o drink,
He'll juist wait till he gets hame,
And peedles in the sink.
Fal-de-dal.

O dinnae worry, Mrs. Johnstone,
My man juist daes the same,
Before he gangs oot tae his wark,
And at nicht when he comes hame,
Sae I staund upon the bairn's stool,
And then turn on the well;
I fling ma kilt richt ower ma heid,
And "P" in the sink masel!
Fal-de-dal.

The Workin Man's Dram

The workin man will hae his dram
Whatever may befaa;
'Tis true, my freens, I tell ye,
The puir man peys for aa.

'Tis a pleasure he has got,
As through life he plods alang,
And yet there's plenty trying
Tae rob him o his dram.

Coal Jock, he is a happy cheil
When he gets on the dot;
'Tis then he is looked down on,
And caaed a drunken sot.

Ye Ministers and Elders,
And Sons o Temperance aa,
There's mony a sair heid gangs tae kirk,
Dressed in their Sunday braw.

There's some wha fairly gulp it doon,
And then dicht oot the gless;
A peppermint drap in their mooth they slap,
Then lock the wee waa press.

Juist gang and lift a shovel and pick,
And toil the hale week lang;
Ye'll then hae very little room
Tae rob him o his dram.

Will ye lift up yer Bible?
And close inspection make,
And ye'll see whaur the Apostle said:
"Take a little for the stomach's sake".

So if we rule by the Holy Book
There isnae muckle wrang;
I dinnae mean tae gang ower far,
But gie a workin man his dram.

Tae An Ingin

Ye dome-shaped juicy-heided lump,
Intae my stomach ye gang plump,
And wi my neive I gied a thump,
Tae ease the pain;
Oot on my cheeks the tears they jump,
Like April rain.

Wi a knife we then slip aff yer tap,
And in a tanker let ye drap,
Then mix ye up wi plenty sap,
Afore ye gaun singin;
Wi a bit o steak, or guid lean nap,
Naethin can beat the ingin.

The guidwife she dances weel aboot,
Searchin, anxious for a clout,
To peel some mair she has a doot,
The pain is stingin!
Wi anger then she stamps her foot,
Aa through slicin up the ingin.

But for a breakfast or a dinner,
Ye cannae get a bite nae finer,
As in the goblet there ye simmer,
Then oh! The smell!
The neebours ken what's yer brimmer,
Brawley they can tell.

And when ye're ready – oh the feed!
We draw the table ower wi speed;
Ye're juist the kind o spread we need,
When freens we're bringin;
We're shuir o a visit frae oor breed,
If we treat them tae an ingin.

For rheumatism, I've heard folks say,
Ye get tae the root without delay,
We hae nae doctor's bill tae pay,
When pains are stingin,
And when we hae a peaceful day,
Oh, hoo we bless the ingin!

When ye were taen frae mither earth,
The place where ye first had birth,
Some thocht ye very little worth,
When infant bulbs were springin,
But we aye grew and showed yer girth,
They praised and loved the ingin.

In Loving Memory of my Old Friend John Todd

Who died on 8th May, 1948.

I've lost a friend, a good old friend.
It has filled my heart with pain,
To part with one I did respect,
I'll never see in life again.

I hope he's gone where good men go.
We were true to one another;
He was the best of company;
I loved him as a brother.

When I look upon that vacant chair,
And think that he is gone:
His kindly face and cheery smile,
My old friend, honest John.

God help those who are left to mourn
To bear their heavy load;
I bid adieu to one so true,
My faithful friend, John Todd.

In Loving Memory of my Old Friend
JOHN TODD
who died on 8th May, 1948.

I've lost a friend, a good old friend :
   It has filled my heart with pain,
To part with one I did respect,
   I'll never see in life again.

I hope he's gone where good men go,
   We were true to one another ;
He was the best of company ;
   I loved him as a brother.

When I look upon that vacant chair,
   And to think that he is gone :
His kindly face and cheery smile,
   My old friend, honest John.

God help those who are left to mourn
   To bear their heavy load ;
I bid adieu to one so true,
   My faithful friend, John Todd.

ROBERT MACLEOD,
Miner Poet.

War

A Jock to his Sweetheart, Nell

or 'Send me oot Some Fags', 1940.

Dear Nell, I'm sitting in my dug-out,
To write ye I tak the chance;
I'm doing my bit wi ither boys
On the battlefields o France.

There's wan thing I miss sair, lassie,
And dinnae you forget;
The cauld it widna bother me,
If I only had a cigarette.

Oh for a whiff o a wee Woodbine,
A Capstan or Gold Flake!
Nae maitter whaur ye get them, Nell,
Send some for puir Jock's sake.

There's plenty smoke oot here, lassie,
As we hide behind sand-bags;
But the reek it has a bad perfume,
It disna smell like fags.

The shells gang booming ower oor heids
As we lie here in the trenches,
Wi our last doupie between oor teeth,
Bletherin aboot fags and wenches.

Then ower we go to face the foe,
Altho he blaws and brags;
Anither victory here we've won;
I think Jock deserves some fags.

So, hurry up and send some oot
Tae yer sodger lad in khaki;
And when I come hame I'll marry you
As shair's my name's Jock Mackie.

The Heroes o Crossgates

Oor collier sodger laddies,
They left the gloomy mine
To fecht for King and country,
They bravely toed the line.

They bade farewell to anes sae dear,
Withoot a sigh or mourn,
To dae their bit wi manly grit,
Maybe never tae return.

They fought like heroes every one,
They did their duty well,
The lads wha donned the khaki,
And fought midst shot and shell.

Some are laid beneath the sod,
Their lives they nobly gave;
For the love of their dear country
They sleep in a soldier's grave.

Some are here amang us noo,
Wi honours tae their name,
Who have bravely fought for freedom
Of Britain's glory and her fame.

Oh, bless the mornin that is gone,
They were oor wee playmates
And we toddled tae schule thegither
Wi the heroes o Crossgates.

In Loving Memory

In loving memory of nurse Catherine Miller and Signaller
J. Steele, the two Dunfermline heroines.

To the core were they true,
Their duty they did do.
Beneath the Red Cross banner,
And the Red, White and Blue.

For the love of their dear country,
The call they did obey,
Went forth to help our comrades
To keep the foe at bay.

Minding the wounded there,
On the battlefields so gory,
Where deeds were done and victories won,
For Britain's fame and glory.

In Heaven's land reward them;
Their lives they nobly gave;
Their names will live amongst us
Though they lie silent in the grave.

IN LOVING MEMORY OF LIEUTENANT W. K. BARCLAY, OF THE 1/7th BLACK WATCH.

Who died of wounds at the hospital in Boulogne, 20th June, 1915.

No more his cheery smile we'll see,
"Our Lieutenant, brave and true;
He died for his King and country
As a hero only can do.

He nobly led his gallant men
'Midst shrapnel, shot, and shell;
While attending to the wounded
Our brave Lieutenant fell.

His native town will miss him much,
Kind friends and comrades all;
He did his duty to the last,
And answered heaven's call.

O, bless those who are left to mourn,
And their burden bravely bear,
And in the realms of heaven above
May they meet their loved one there.

BY ROBERT MACLEOD.

79 Union Street, Cowdenbeath.

Clipping from an unnamed newspaper.

My Brother

My last tribute to my dear brother who was killed in the
Great War.

He died amidst the shot and shell,
Our brother, brave and true;
We little thought it was the last,
When he bade us that fond adieu.

His manly form, his smiling face,
In life again I will never see,
But the little photo that adorns the wall
Will always be treasured by me.

Sad was our home when the letter was read,
With his pals he fell in the fray;
He gave his young life for his country,
In fighting for liberty.

Though far away in a foreign land
He sleeps in a soldier's grave,
We can only say, with sorrowing hearts,
He has fallen with the brave.

The Heroes of Moeuvres

Corporal David Hunter and six comrades of the 1st / 5th. Battalion
H.L.I. 52nd Division, who made that brave stand at Moeuvres,
17th and18th September 1918.[6]

Heroes to the core were they,
And did their duty well;
They kept the snarling Hun at bay,
Midst flying shot and shell.

Brave Corporal Hunter led them on,
That heroic little band;
He cried, "Our duty must be done",
As he stood there in command.

Stand by your guns, my faithful ones,
Be Britons brave and true!
We'll fight for right and show the Huns
What British pluck can do.

They nobly faced the fierce attack,
From their post could not be driven,
And boldly kept the Germans back,
The daring dauntless seven.

---

[6] David F. Hunter (1891–1965) was awarded the Victoria Cross for outstanding
bravery and his comrades were awarded the Military Medal. He was
promoted to sergeant, and at the end of the war returned to Dunfermline and
to his life as a miner. Hunter's photo is in the Imperial War Museum, <www.
iwm.org.uk/collections/item/object/205297034>

Till reinforcements they drew nigh,
That gallant stand was made
By the heroes of the H.L.I.
May their colours never fade.

We'll touch our cap to those heroes all,
And give them hearty cheers;
They stood as firmly as a wall,
Those heroes of Moeuvres.

The Gallant Guards' Return

A hearty return ye stalwart sons,
Your duty you have done,
At Mons and bloody Festuebert
Good laurels you have won.

At Neuve Chapelle midst shot and shell
You stemmed the German tide,
With bomb and glittering bayonet
You stood grimly side by side.

The Grenadiers, Coldstreams and Scots,
The Welsh, and Irish too,
Have done their bit with manly grit
As Britons can only do.

Bravo, good Old Contemptibles[7]
You were ready tae a man
To lift the gun and toe the line,
Or follow in the van.

And those who love their native land
Can tell his little story;
How the Guards sternly did fight
On the field for British glory.

---

[7] 'The Old Contemptibles' was the name adopted by British troops who survived World War One.

A Welcome Home

To the boys who have come back from the war (1914–1918.)

Home from the blood-stained battlefields
Our true and gallant men,
Back to the land they love dearly
The mountain and the glen,
They've bravely faced the mighty foe
And done their duty well,
And fought on to the bitter end
Midst shrapnel shot and shell.

Many have died for their country's sake
And did it with a will,
They gave their lives so freely
That we may live in freedom still.
Many have honours to their names
For good service they have done,
With manly grit they did their bit
In battles fought and won.

A mother stands in her cottage door
With sad and weeping eyes,
And cries, "Oh! God my son, my son,"
With heart-broken heavy sighs
A husband meets his loving wife
First time for many years,
His little boy his pride and joy
And all are bathed in tears.

A sister kisses his wan cheek
A token of fond love,
He presses her to his breast
A kind lesson from above.
They speak of days of long ago
When they learned the golden rule,
The happy days of childhood
When at the village school.

A sweetheart greets her soldier lad
To prove her love once more,
He tells her of his thoughts of home
While fighting on a distant shore.
A brother meets a brother true
And gives him a welcome hand,
How proud of him who nobly led
His brave and gallant band.

So let us rally round the boys
And give them a hearty cheer,
And say a warm "Welcome Home"
To those we cherish so dear,
And when their time is up to go
Let us shout with might and main,
And wish them God-speed and good luck
Till they return home again.

A WELCOME HOME.

To The Boys who have come back.

Home from the blood-stained battle fields
  Our true and gallant men,
Back to the land they love dearly
  The mountain and the glen.
They've bravely faced the mighty foe
  And did their duty well,
And fought on to the bitter end
  'Midst shrapnel shot and shell.

Many have died for their country's sake
  And did it with a will,
They gave their lives so freely
  That we may live in freedom still.
Many have honours to their names
  For good service they have done,
With manly grit they did their bit
  In battles fought and won.

A mother stands in her cottage door
  With sad and weeping eyes,
And cries Oh! God my son, my son
  With heart-broken heavy sighs.
A husband meets his loving wife
  The first for many years,
His little boy his pride and joy
  And all are bathed in tears.

A sister kisses his wan cheek
  A token of fond love,
He presses her to his breast
  A kind lesson from above.
They speak of days long ago
  When they learned the golden rule,
The happy days of childhood
  When at the village school.

A sweetheart greets her soldier lad
  To prove her love once more,
He tells her of his thoughts of home
  While fighting on a distant shore.
A brother meets a brother true
  And gives him a welcome hand
How proud of him who nobly led
  His brave and gallant band.

So let us rally round the boys
  And give them a hearty cheer,
And say a warm " Welcome Home "
  To those we cherish so dear,
And when their time is up to go
  Let us shout with might and main,
And wish them God-speed and good luck
  Till they return home again.

Robert Macleod,
Miner Poet.

169 Union Street,
Cowdenbeath.

PETER WATT, PRINTER, COWDENBEATH.

Britons to the Last

Written in 1939.

Britons again have been provoked,
The call to arms rings through our land,
Once more our lads in deadly conflict,
Side by side will take their stand,
When the foe is to face us,
We are ready to do or die,
When the word of command is given,
And we hear the battle cry.

Tribute tae the 51st Highland Division

The Fifty-first Division
The lads o great fame;
Frae the tap tae the toe,
We ken they are game.

For when they start charging,
The Huns tak tae their heels;
They are feared at the lads
Wi their bayonets o steel.

When robbed o their rifle,
They fecht wi their mitts;
When they get guid Scotch room,
They soon polish aff Fritz.

It is born within them
Tae ne'er shirk frae the foe;
But where there is fechtin,
Side by side they will go.

Wi the swing o the tartan,
When they hear the pipes lilt,
They drive hame the bayonet,
Aye, richt up tae the hilt.

They rush on like wild stag,
Gie them it hot and pell-mell;
Nae wonder they caa them
The mad women frae Hell.

The foemen they dread them,
May their courage ne'er fade,
The starkest o fechters,
Oor brave Highland Brigade.   Written in 1942.

The Nazi 'Hell-Ship'

The Altmark, Feb. 16, 1940.[8]

Down in the dark dreary hold
Our gallant seamen lay,
Away from God's pure fresh air
And cheery light of day.

Imprisoned by a heartless crew,
A cruel and treacherous foe,
Treated like the savage beast,
In the dungeon down below.

When off the coast of Norway
Sailed that floating hell,
With true and sturdy seamen
Their sad story now can tell.

The snow-clad hills of Norway
In their memories will ever live,
Who for the good old Union Jack
Their lives would freely give.

But the hearts of our brave sailors
Who never yet gave way,
But helped each other in their cause,
As in the filthy prison lay.

---

[8] The 'Altmark' was a German prison ship transporting 299 British merchant seamen, all imprisoned in the hold. Off the coast of Norway it was intercepted by HMS Cossack. The prisoners were liberated and all brought back to Scotland.

When sighted by the "Cossack",
With speed went to their aid,
When on the awful "Hell-Ship"
A daring dash was made.

"Come on, my gallant heroes,"
Our Naval Officer did cry,
With hand- to hand in fighting
They were ready to do-or-die.

We'll touch our caps to the heroes all,
Those true and faithful ones,
Who did their duty, every man
Like hard fighting British sons.

The Men of El Alamein

Written in October 1943.

Bravo! Ye men of El Alamein,
The Eigth Army of fighting fame,
Lads of grit they did their bit
And Rommel's hordes they did outwit.

Wi Camerons, Seaforths and Argylls
They drove the Jerries back for miles,
With gallant Gordons and Black Watch
The foemen knew they'd met their match.

They came from the mountain and the glen
Our brave-hearted fighting men;
The Desert Rats were keen of scent
Into the fray like wild-stag went.

Our Infantry were firm and sound,
Better tank-busters couldn't be found;
The 40th and 50th did their share,
The shouts of victory filled the air.

Men of courage didn't lack,
The treacherous foe were driven back;
And "Monty" trusted in his men
For the turning point at El Alamein.

Lads I'm proud of you today,
Kind providence has led the way;
We fought to conquer with a will
That truth and justice would prevail.

To beat the foe was their ambition
The sturdy lads of the Highland Division;
Let us touch our caps once again
To the men who fought at El Alamein.[9]

---

[9] In 1942 the Second Battle of El Alamein took place between 23 October and 11 November, near the Egyptian railway halt of El Alamein . Montgomery had taken command of the British Eighth Army and this victory turned the tide in the North African Campaign, marking a major turning point in the Western Desert Campaign of the Second World War.

The Great Arctic Battle

The Sinking of the Scharnhorst, December 1943.

The mighty Scharnhorst now lies low
Under the surging waves,
We showed the Huns our motto:
Britons never shall be slaves.

To stop our convoy she was bound,
In the mists of that Arctic sea,
Our cruiser Norfolk dealt a blow,
Then a shattered wreck was she.

Then broadside came the Duke of York,
With seamen loyal and true,
The Belfast and the Sheffield,
With their lads in navy blue.

The German seamen were no match
For the boys of bulldog breed,
Who worked the guns to beat the Huns,
In their dishonoured creed.

Our destroyers Savage and Scorpion,
Suarez and Norwegian Stord,
That fought with might and main,
With manly hearts aboard.

The Jamaica struck the final blow,
That fatal torpedo sped,
And sent the Scharnhorst to her doom,
In the hellish ocean bed.

Brave Admiral Sir Bruce Fraser,
You officers and gallant men;
The pride of German Navy,
Will never fight again.

National and International
Events

A Tribute To King Edward

To the memory of our late sovereign King Edward
'The Peacemaker'.[10]

A tribute from a few loyal subjects in Cowdenbeath.

The nation mourns at its loss,
Another King has gone;
Gone for ever to dwell with Him,
Who sits upon the Throne.

O death thou art a mystery,
The peacemaker to us all;
For it will come we know not when,
So be ready for the call.

The God above who rules us all,
He takes what he has given;
The rich, the poor, we must all go,
To meet our King in Heaven.

---

[10] Born in 1841, Edward ('Bertie') was the eldest son of Queen Victoria and Prince Albert. In 1863 he married Alexandra of Denmark (daughter of the King of Denmark) and after Queen Victoria's death in 1901, he became King Edward VII. He died in 1910.

In Memory of Captain Scott

> Captain Scott who perished at the South Pole, March 1912
> with members of the Terra Nova team. Captain Scott's ship
> was called The Terra Nova.

Bring down the flag to half mast high,
Ye hardy sons of Britain, weep,
For the heroes brave across the wave,
Who now in polar regions sleep.

On board the 'Terra Nova'
Our heroes did set sail,
But not a single soul of them
Was left to tell the tale.

In the wild wastes of the Antarctic,
Where that dreadful blizzard blew,
There perished our gallant explorer,
Captain Scott and his brave crew.

In the prime of life and height of fame
He died like a hero brave,
His deeds will be kept in memory
Though now silent in the grave.

The Titanic

Written in 1912.

On the fourteenth of April
      at early break of day,
The gallant ship "Titanic" sailed
      merrily on her way,
It was her maiden voyage
      and all supposed that she,
Would reach her destination
      but it was not to be.

The Captain did his best to save
      the vessel's human load,
But found it was beyond his power,
      it was the will of God,
That many there should perish
      beneath the surging waves,
Unconscious just two hours before
      that God had planned their graves.

Heroes of the Air

The Atlantic flight by H. G. Hawker and Commander K.
MacKenzie Grieve, RN. who made that gallant attempt on
18th May 1919 in a Sopwith Scout.

From the shores of Newfoundland our airmen did leave,
Daring Harry Hawker and Commander Grieve.
They boarded the Sopwith, their great aeroplane,
And flew away like joy-birds above their surging main.

With full speed ahead the engine did rattle,
Through fog, mist, and rain they bravely did battle,
When the filter pipe choked, trouble came their way,
While fathoms below a watery grave lay.

The red light in mid-ocean showed they were in distress,
"Is it Hawker?" was signalled, the answer came "Yes",
Oh kind was dear "Mary" to her skipper and crew,[11]
To be there by your side, what more could they do?

On the shores of Bonnie Scotland they safely did stand,
While cheers of great joy did ring through the land;
Health to Hawker and Grieve, with endless delight,
Let us wish them good luck in their next aerial flight!

---

[11] The SS Mary was the Danish steamship responsible for rescuing the
aviators, then bringing them safely to Scotland.

The Great Atlantic Flight

Flight accomplished by Captain J. Alcock, D.S.C. and
navigator, Lieut. A. Whitton Brown 14/15th June, 1919.

From Newfoundland shores they waved farewell,
Our airmen brave and true,
They entered their Vickers-Vimy machine
And faced the ocean blue.

Soon 'midst the clouds they were whirling,
Soaring beneath a hazy sky,
With good courage and adventure
The great Atlantic then to fly.

With spirits bright and following breeze,
Confident their power would stay,
They sought to fly that awful span,
To the hidden zone far away.

They set the engines at full speed,
They knew they had a task,
And pulled along with might and main-
To reach Clifden at last.

All honour to Alcock and Brown,
May their hearts be gay and light;
We'll give three cheers for our airmen
Who did that non-stop flight.

Tribute to the Memory of the Queen Mother[12]

The nation mourns at her loss,
Our Queen Mother she is gone;
Gone for ever to dwell with them
Who sing around the throne.

She was a loving, gentle Queen,
With a mother's tender love;
Mingled with the poor in distress,
May she wear a crown above.

When death it gives the fatal blow,
As it cometh to us all;
The rich, the poor, the weak, and strong,
Lord prepare us for the call.

Oh! God above, our creator,
He takes what He has given;
Our good Queen Mother calmly sleeps,
Let her soul now rest in heaven.

---

[12] Written on the death of Alexandra, mother of King George V, Nov. 20, 1925. She was the daughter-in-law of Queen Victoria, as she was married to Victoria and Albert's eldest son, Edward VII, who was king from 1901 to 1910. On his death, their son George V became king, and Alexandra became Queen Mother.

To the Memory of King George V

To the memory of our late beloved sovereign King George
V (1865–1936).[13] A tribute from a few loyal subjects of
Cowdenbeath. (R.MacL.)

Our monarch he has gone to rest,
The nation she has shed her tears,
Yet still his kindly deeds will live,
Throughout the coming years.

To us he ruled as one so true,
Beloved by great and small
Our sailor King now laid low
Has obeyed his Maker's call.

O calm and peaceful be his sleep,
A promise sure is given,
To bless those who are left to mourn,
May he dwell with saints in Heaven.

---

[13] Son of Edward VII, King George V was born in 1865. He was monarch from
1910 till is death in 1936.

Love and Affection

Bonnie Wee Nell o Spinkie Dell

I loved a wee lass as dear as my life,
Oft times we promised tae become man and wife,
But she vanished from memory, sad story I'll tell –
Often she gathered the wild flowers around Spinkie Dell.

Tae the school we toddled each hand in hand,
And wi oor wee playmates we joined in the band;
When lessons were oer, at the toll o the bell,
We hastened away tae dear auld Spinkie Dell.

And there we did ramble till the oor it got late,
Telling childish love, me and my wee mate;
We gathered the daises, foxgloves and bluebells,
That grew in their beauty around Spinkie Dell.

Then hame we did wander as the sun gaed tae rest,
That tinted the sky in far golden west;
'Twas then that we did pairt, and bade oor farewell,
No more did we roam around Spinkie Dell.

In summer the children crowned the May Queen,
And decked her fair brow with ivy so green,
But my treasure is gone that I loved so well,
And there's no joy for me now around Spinkie Dell.

Then stricken with fever in cold death she lay,
And tae the old churchyard they took her away;
At the fall of the leaf I lost my wee Nell –
How dreary it looks now around Spinkie Dell.

The woods o Blairadam in splendour may bloom,
And birds tae me may lilt their sweet tune;
Oh! cruel was the blow as on me it fell,
And picked from me my blossom o dear Spinkie Dell.

May the angels in heaven list tae my prayer,
And keep my wee Nell in their tender care,
Till we meet up above where saints do dwell;
For her sake I will wander around Spinkie Dell.

By Eden's Stream

By Eden's muted enchanted stream,
Where soft the crystal waters glide,
Fair as a vision in a dream,
My lovely Mary does reside.
There duly oft at dewy eve,
My gentle Mary roves with me,
When sleeping nature seems to breathe,
The soul of love and poesy.

How sweet with her to dwell,
Far from the city's gloomy shade,
And every day by field and fell,
To rove with my sweet Lowland maid.
Ere morning broke among the hills,
We'd lead our flocks by dale and dean,
And drink the nectar of the rills,
And rest on Nature's carpet green.

Still as I gaze upon those charms,
Fresh as a rose just newly blown,
Her beauty all my bosom warms,
With raptures all before unknown,
Within yon out by Eden's stream,
With gentle Mary as my bride,
Life would be an enchanted dream,
If there with her I might abide.

Clapperbum Raw

Locally known by that name.

There's a spot dear tae me in our mining toun,
When I look back on the years that's awaa!
We played aa thegither like birds o a feather
At this place they caaed "Clapperbum Raw".

Hoo it got that name, this wee spot o fame,
It's kent by true freens far awaa!
They wad gie aa they claim tae be back again
Tae get a sicht o auld "Clapperbum Raw".

It's noo aa forlorn, the waas they are worn,
It has stood mony a blast o winter's snaw;
Oft my lessons I did learn when I was a bairn
Roon the fireside in auld "Clapperbum Raw".

We played at the dyke tae oor hert's delight,
At hide and seek, the game we loved braw;
Wi wee Charlie Greig we played 'smuggle the geg'
Roon the corner at auld "Clapperbum Raw".

We toddled tae school, and this was the rule,
Tae obey our parents what e'er may befaa,
And aye keep in mind tae yin anither be kind
Like guid playmates at auld "Clapperbum Raw".

There was Robbie and Bennie, Willie and Teenie,
And Sandy Broon like a saft Johnnie Raw;
He wad haud out his hand and the pammies wad stand
For the dunces o auld "Clapperbum Raw".

'Twas there I coorted Jean, I thocht her a queen;
On Sundays she dressed up clean and braw;
Her bonnie fair hair, there's few can compare
Wi my lassie in auld "Clapperbum Raw".

Noo I'm aged and grey, but still spunk and gay,
But those bright happy days I recaa,
When I stood by her side, my lovely young bride,
We were mairrit at auld "Clapperbum Raw".

"CLAPPERBUM RAW."

Locally known by that name.

There's a spot dear to me in oor mining toon
  Wnen I look back on the years that's awa :
We played a' the gither like birds o' a feather
  at this place they ca'd "Clapperbum Raw."

Hoo it got that name, this wee spot o' fame,
  But it's kent by true freens far awa :
They wad gie a' they claim to be back again
  To get a sicht o' auld "Clapperbum Raw."

It's noo a' forlorn, the wa's they are worn,
  It had stood mony a blast o' winter's snaw :
Oft' my lessons I did learn when I was a bairn
  Roon' the fireside in auld "Clapperbum Raw."

We played at the dyke to oor hert's delight,
  At hide-and-seek, the game we love'd braw :
Wi' wee Charlie Greig we played smuggle the geg
  Roon' the corner at auld "Clapperbum Raw."

We toddled to school, and this was the rule,
  To obey oor parents what e'er may befa',
And aye keep in mind to yin anither be kind
  Like guid playmates at auld "Clapperbum Raw."

There was Robbie and Bennie, Willie and Teenie,
  And Sandy Broon like a saft Johnnie Raw :
He wad haud oot his hand and the pammies wad stand
  For the dunces o' auld "Clapperbum Raw."

'Twas there I coorted Jean, I thocht her a queen ;
  On Sunday's she dressed up clean and braw :
Her bonnie fair hair, there's few can compare
  Wi' my lassie in auld "Clapperbum Raw."

Noo I'm aged and grey, but still spunk and gay,
  But those bright happy days I reca',
When I stood by her side, my lovely young bride,
  We were marrit at auld "Clapperbum Raw."

169 Union Street,   ROBERT MacLEOD
  Cowdenbeath   Miner Poet.

Football

Cowden's Daein Fine

Oor team are getting aff their mark,
The lads in blue at Central Park,
They're fairly warming tae their work,
Cowden's daein fine.

When awaa in mony a game,
They've had hard luck aa the same,
But if they get the pints at hame,
Cowden's daein fine.

Wi Neil, oor goalie, and sturdy backs,
A half back line we hae the cracks,
They'll gie mony a team their whacks,
Cowden's daein fine.

A forward line when on the rin,
Wi men like Ross and centre Quinn,
They can fairly bang them in,
Cowden's daein fine.

As the cup ties are drawin near,
We'll greet them wi a cheer,
And shout like mad when they appear,
Aye, Cowden's daein fine.

Willie Devlin on the Baa

O aa the centres I like the best,
There's ane I fancy abune the rest,
Gey often he has stood the test –
Willie Devlin on the baa,

Since he came tae Central Park,
On the cross-bars he's left his mark;
Ye ken he warms tae his wark
When he gets on the baa.

Against the Celts last Setturday,
Hoo weel oor lads in blue did play,
But yin I mean wha paved the way
Was Devlin on the baa.

Wee Pullar put on number wan,
As doon the wing he beat his man,
Then he thocht it was his plan
Tae get Devlin on the baa.

When the second half it did begin,
'Twas then he fairly banged them in,
There wis nae chance for wee Shevlin
Wi Devlin on the baa.

Auld McNair had juist tae look,
He said, "That centre kens his book,"
The third, a bonnie goal, he took,
Willie Devlin on the baa.

We hope he aye keeps up his score,
Wi twenty-nine goals he cries for more;
When the season ends we'll cry "Encore!"
For Devlin on the baa.

In Loving Memory of John McArthur

Died at Hampden Park on 8th October 1949.

He died in the hour of victory,
A true sport to the end:
Beloved throughout the football world;
A loyal and faithful friend.

To see his team triumphant,
It was his great desire;
But when that fatal goal was scored,
His life it did expire.

He's gone; oh, silent be his rest
Till heaven bells do toll!
May we meet our good friend John
At that eternal goal.

Keep Cowden at the Tap

Bravo good old Cowden,
They're daein weel the noo,
A team o triers aa the time,
The lads who wear the blue.
They work in best o harmony,
And play wi grit and snap,
So we're aa prood tae see,
Auld Cowden at the tap.

Wi Shaw between the goalposts,
He can fairly clear,
Duncan and Brown are the backs,
In them there is nae fear,
Hardie, Erskine and Murray,
Ken maist every gap,
They're helping aa they can,
Tae keep Cowden at the tap.

And then there is the forward line,
They are a sturdy lot,
Wi Marshall and Simpson on the right,
They're aye upon the dot,
And Frankie Quinn, oor centre,
At goal he likes a pap,
He tangles up the centre halves,
Tae keep Cowden at the tap.

And noo we come tae the left-wing,
They are a clever pair,
For Reid and Beckett's passing moves,
Hae defences in despair.
Not least there's manager Dougary,
He'll never let them drap,
We'll support them weel upon the field,
And keep Cowden at the tap.

Sandy Ye're A Dandy

There's a player wha fairly taks the ee
A guid yin noo ye'll aa agree,
On the baa he's a treat tae see
O Sandy, he's a dandy!
The wey that he can dance aboot,
And bangs the baa wi either foot,
Nae wonder the spectators shout,
Sandy, ye're a dandy!

O Sandy, ye're a dandy
O Sandy, ye're a don,
Ye come in awfu handy
As goals are pilin on,
Wi yer tricky little touches
As guid as e'er we saw,
We've outside richts in Scotland,
But ye're the dandy o them aa.

Fifteen years ye've been at Rangers noo,
And donned the colours bonnie blue,
And aye proved sae staunch and true –
O Sandy, ye're a dandy.
Tae see ye prancing doon the wing
And get the baa on the swing,
 Mony a braw goal it does bring –
O Sandy ye're a dandy!

The Goal-keeper's Ghost

Parody on 'Tam O' Shanter.'

When chaps and cronies on the street,
Can hardly staun upon their feet,
When this yin's wat and that yin's dry,
And no a star in aa the sky,
When hail and snaw and sleet combine,
Ilka drap that faas that wad fill a byne,
On sic a nicht I taen the road.
Encumbered wi a heavy load.
O mountain dew I had my share,
And wondered whaur I'd get some mair,
The lamps shone feeble in the gloom,
And aa was silent as the tomb.
No even a body on the street,
Except the bobby on his beat,
But wat or dry it's aa the same,
They're there tae tak the wanderer hame.

I passed that bobby like a man,
And juist wi that the clock struck wan,
Little I care for the man in blue,
That very nicht, I'm telling you.

My thochts were aa aboot the wife,
Wha often said she'd tak my life,
And yon yin that I hae can growl,
Or decorate ye wi a bowl.
Auld Glesca whom nae toon surpasses,
For fighting wifies and cunning lasses,
And chaps that preach and live gey fat:
Of coorse by sendin roon the hat

Still staggerin on I bravely went,
I riped my pouches, no a cent,
Except the scent was in my nose,
And that's no muckle I suppose.

I leaned my heid against the waa,
And just wi that the clock struck twaa,
But later on strange sounds I heard,
When passin by the auld kirkyaird.
It was a kirkyaird kent tae me,
But hang the tombstone I could see,
My heid, I think, began tae reel,
That graveyaird looked a fitbaa field.

There stood the goalposts gaping wide,
And there the players, eleven-a-side,
And crutches there for every man,
Forbye a ghaistly ambulance van,
Wan goalkeeper there did staun,
A fireclay brick held in each haun,
The ither yin business meant an aa,
Held in his fist a jiner's saw.

But wha was referee? I looked –
A tail he had and horns sae crooked,
I glowered – gey funny I did feel,
It was his "Nibs" himsel, the Deil.
The game began, the baa did flee,
And juist wi that the clock struck three,
Then fast and furious waxed the fun,
About the field the players did run.

The forwards dodged, the backs were guid,
Nae maiter what the half-backs did,
He couldna kick a fitbaa through,
Till wan wee fella fairly flew,
Right doon the wing and banged the baa,
But it struck the centre on the paw,
And then the goalkeeper wi the saw,
Left his trade mark on his jaw.

Half-time, the game again begun,
Spectators flocked into the grun,
They shairly left their graves that nicht,
Aa ghosts, they were an eerie sicht,
They yelled and egged the players on,
And some did cheer, and some did groan,
"A foul! A foul!" was their next yell,
Agreed by auld "Nicolas" himsel.

The whistle blew, the foul allooed,
Which seemed tae satisfy the crood,
Bang went the baa, it fairly flew,
Aa roared at yince, "It's through, it's through!"
"It's no through yet," I did remark,
And in an instant, aa was dark,
At me the ghostly gang did glower,
And juist wi that the clock struck fower.

"Ah, Tam! Ah, Tam! Ye'll get yer fairin,
As shair as guns are made o airn!"
That was their cry, next thing I feel,
The ghostly gang was at my heels,
And foremost, tae, among them aa,
Was the goalkeeper wi his glitterin saw.

I ran doon the road and ower the burn,
He followed me at every turn.
I couldnae stop, I couldnae speak,
I felt his braith upon my cheek,
Fast, aye faster on we gaed,
Near an nearer on me he made.
He raised the saw and gied a laugh,
And then I found ma ears cut aff!

"Whaur am I noo? Come tell me quick!"
A voice replied, "Ye're in the nick",
"We thocht ye'd never come alive",
An juist wi that the clock struck five,
For lang I thocht, I'm in a fix,
Whit time is it noo? We slop at six.
I wondered if I was really livin,
A bonnie breakfast I was givin
Wi a scone as hard as ony plate,
Nae wonder then clock chap't eight.

They marched me oot tae toe the line,
As the court-hoose clock wis striking nine,
A guinea or fourteen days, and then,
The Black Maria arrived at ten.
It wis nae use o me deceivin,
We reached Barlinnie aboot eleiven,
I got a bath, I nivver shall,
Forget, for then the clock struck twall.

To the Memory of John Thomson

Cardenden miner and international footballer, who died at
Ibrox, Sept. 5, 1931, age 22.

We've lost John Thomson, our goalkeeper so grand,
No more by the uprights his manly figure will stand,
Beloved by his clubmates and friends on every side,
To do his duty well, poor John took a pride.

Oh! that daring save which cost him his life,
How he dashed so his club would win in the strife,
To keep his goal from downfall, he fell at his post,
And a true friend and sportsman to the game has been lost.

His name will live on the field of play,
Where he gave many a gallant display,
And, when the ball does cease to roll,
May we meet him at that eternal goal.

Scotland

Girls feeding Peacocks in the Glen 1925

Gala Day in Pittencrieff Park 1907

Dunfermline's Bonnie Glen

I am a simple collier chiel,
And o aa joys I ken.
There's naething I like better
Than a stroll through Dunfermline Glen.

The trees wi foliage green and gay,
The wee birds in the pen,
Aa help tae mak up the beauty
O Dunfermline's bonnie Glen.

It was gien by Andrew Carnegie,
A son o the auld grey toon,
Wha wis brocht up amang us,
A hard-working, canny loon.

In Moodie Street where he wis born,
And grew clever wi the pen,
He noo gies us oor pleasure
In Dunfermline's bonnie Glen.

Tae tak a walk in an afternoon
And listen tae the band,
And sit tae oor heart's content
In front o the bandstand.

The gardens arrayed in splendour
Wi lovely flouers ye ken,
The perfume's rare in the hothouses there
In Dunfermline's bonnie Glen.

The Pittencrieff Hoose, baith clean and braw,
Decked wi its coat o white,
And oor loyal son's statue on the brae,
Is a pleasure tae the sight.

Children jumpin aboot wi joy,
Waitin their turn on a swing,
They tak it very sad at hert
When the departin hour does ring.

So when ye're visitin the Auld Grey Toon,
If ye hae an hour tae len
Just daunner doon an see the sicht
In Dunfermline's bonnie Glen.

In Memory o Rabbie Burns

Oh! Rabbie, man, ye little ken
Hoo muckle thocht o ye are by men;
Men o high and low degree,
Even a miner bard like me.

Had ye been ayeways tae the fore,
'Tis you I'm shair they wad adore,
But oor plooman bard is lang syne deid,
And a cauld, cauld stane noo haps his heid.

When ye wandered by Nith's winding stream
Wi yer bairns and bonnie Jean;
A loving wife wi a hamely smile
Wha loved the lad born in Kyle.

Amang the clods when ye were ploo'in,
The moosie's nest wis sent a-strewin;
It wis turned oot o hoose and haa,
But still ye had a love for aa.

Ye loved the bonnie banks o Doon,
In summer time when aa in bloom,
The birds, the flouers, and scented breeze,
And robins sang amang the trees.

Yer noble works we love tae read
And think upon yer noble heid,
Hoo ye hae penned line efter line,
And put them in the best o rhyme.

But we will praise the lad o mirth,
And each year celebrate his birth;
Auld Scotland's sons wi sorrow mourns,
For their ain dear poet, Rabbie Burns.

Oor Ain Toons

Kirkcaldy's famous for its smell;
It fairly makes things hum,
So if your gas mask you'd try oot,
Ye ken the place tae come.

Linoleum is Kirkcaldy's pride,
Tae make it they work hard,
And though it's worn by the "foot",
They sell it by the "yard".

Now Auchtermuchty is a sma toon;
It's famous for its station,
But better known for miles aroon
For its funny pronunciation.

Kinross on bonnie Loch Leven stands,
Where mony a boatie sails;
But it is far more famous,
For all its "fishy" tales.

Then Perth is Scotland's beauty spot,
Between two "Inches" lying
And lots o folk in it reside
Who keep alive by "dyeing".

In Scotland there are lots o birds:
There's sparrows, craws and seagulls,
The golfers on St Andrews course
Are shooting at "Gleneagles".

And Montrose beside the silver sea,
Where the wee white baa aye jinks,
There mony a pair that hae been matched,
Living sweethearts tied in links.

The Kirkcaldy Esplanade

Oor esplanade is brawly made,
Oh! What a grand construction;
And visitors noo, frae far and near,
Find it a great attraction.

We thank the Corporation o the toon
For how it has been laid,
The gangers and the workers aa
Wha wrocht on the Esplanade.

Tae hae a walk on an afternoon
And smell the saut sea air,
And tak a seat, it's just a treat,
It drives awaa dull care.

Yon big sea waa it looks sae braw,
As the breakers they are dashin,
The bairns tae, they jump wi glee,
When they see the waves come splashin.

They love tae romp upon the sands,
And in the sea tae wade,
Then supple up their little legs
Along the Esplanade.

'Tis there you get a car or bus
Aa standing ready made,
Tae tak ye ony place ye like
Frae oor ain Esplanade.

I hope my rhyme will please ye fine,
As I'm juist a miner laddie,
On what I've said aboot the Esplanade.
In the Lang Toon o Kirkcaldy.

The Bonnie Isle o Skye[14]

I love the bonnie Isle o Skye;
O that wee bit land I am proud
With its ancient Dunvegan Castle
The seat of the MacLeods –
The home of our brave clansmen
In days long, long gone by;
My heart it warms dearly to
The bonnie Isle o Skye.

The rippling waters of Loch Scavaig,
A pleasure to the sight,
A scene to live in memory,
To the soul a pure delight,
The lovely glens and lofty bens
Of the Cuillins, towering high;
They all make up the beauties
O the bonnie Isle o Skye.

---

[14] The poem was published in *The Clarion of Skye*, Issue 53, June 1955

Skye Children's Corner

Rory Ban

By CALUM NICOLSON

One of the best known shepherds in the north west of Skye was Rory Ban. He was for many years employed on the Ollisdale hirsell of the Glendale estate. I happened to be fishing on the Ollisdale loch in 1920 when I met Rory. He was a happy-go-lucky kind of a man, and as harmless as a lamb. He was about fifty years of age. In his younger days he was a great shinty player and no shinty match was complete without him. Rory approached me with a broad smile on his face, and said, I thought you was one of the club, Calum. What club, I said. The mountain club, said Rory. I asked Rory if he got many visitors in his lonely glen. Ach yes Calum, I met a good looking lady here last week. She stopped and said, good morning Donald, I am sure you are a long way off from here on a fine day. I said, ach yes, my lady. Perhaps as far as Glasgow, she said. Ach yes and much farther, my lady. Perhaps as far as London, she said. Ach yes, and much farther, I told her. Perhaps as far as America then, she said. Oh yes, and much farther than America, my lady. Well, what do you think Calum, she put her face next to mine and said in a low voice, now Donald, tell me true, how far can you see anyway? I said to her, ach. my lady, if its a clear night I can see as far as the moon. When she

heard this she gave me a queer look, picked up her haversack and walked away without saying good-bye. I think she must have been one of those that's always looking for a soft man, Calum. Only a month ago I met a young student here collecting samples of soil. He told me he was taking it to St Andrew's Hotel in Edinburgh for the high-ups to see if this place was suitable for growing coco-nuts and tobacco. A few days ago I met another student here who was from the same place. He asked me if I knew where he could get some nice stones. I told him to go down to the MacLeod's Maidens when the tide was out and he would get plenty nice stones. I warned him to watch that the tide did not cut him off. Ach well, he must have fallen in love with the Maidens for he never came back. I get plenty of visitors of that kind, but I also get visitors who are generous and kind.

I was sorry to hear that Rory had passed on, a few years before the last war, and that his collie dog Glen was the chief mourner at his master's funeral.

THE GOOD BOOK SAYETH:

That ye may be blameless and harmless, the sons of God, without rebuke, in the midst of a crooked and perverse nation, among whom ye shine as lights in the world. Phillipians—Chap. 2-15 verse.

Use your talent for God's glory, and He will give you more to use. Do the little duties faithfully and you will grow in skill and ability, and be able for greater. No duties are small or unimportant. There are many who grow discouraged because they are kept all their lives at little tasks. Men praise grand and heroic deeds, and little heroisms of daily duty. But you remember what one said—That if God sent two angels to earth, one to rule an empire and the other to clean a street, they would each regard their employment as equally distinguished. True faithfulness regards nothing as small or unimportant. So if any of you little children when you grow up get an important position or a place of honour among your kind—remember not to put on airs when in the presence of those not so fortunate as you, for humility is a sign of breeding, culture and christianity.

Editor.

■■
■■

Bonnie Isle of Skye

I love the bonnie Isle of Skye;
O' that wee bit land I'm proud,
With its ancient Dunvegan Castle;
The seat of the MacLeods.
The home of our brave clansmen,
In days long, long gone by;
My heart it warms dearly,
To the bonnie Isle of Skye.

The rippling waters of Loch
Scavaig
A pleasure to the sight.
A scene, to live in memory:
To the soul a pure delight.
The lovely glens and lofty bens
Of the Cuillions towering high;
They all make up the beauties
O' the bonnie Isle of Skye.

ROBERT MacLEOD.
Cowdenbeath.

The Loch Ness Monster

The Loch Ness "monster" what can it be,
A whale or shark cam frae the sea?
Nae mortal soul can really say,
Intae the loch it has found its way.

'Tis there some folks will exclaim,
Although they cannae tell its name;
Maybe it's juist a floating tree,
Or a guid keg o barley bree.

If that's the case, the feat wad be risky,
Tae first-fit him wi a bottle of whisky;
But wi ye he micht no be ceivil
If he happened tae be a deep-sea deivil!

Or if Jonah was in his belly,
Ye then would meet this long lost fellae;
In his hidin place a line I'd set,
Then slip him gently intae a net.

It's puittin the countryside in fear,
Hundreds tae the loch dae steer,
Tae get a glimpse o this big stranger
That's causin aa this strife and danger.

If we could only find oot his creek,
Wha's playin wi us hide-and-seek;
What can it be? We are left tae guess,
But we hope tae catch the "monster" o Loch Ness.

Philosophy and Nature

Keep on, Keep on

If the day looks kind o gloomy
And the chances kind o slim,
If the situation's puzzlin,
And the prospects awfu grim.

And perplexities keep pressing
Till all hope is nearly gone,
Just pluck up and grit yer teeth
And keep on, keep on.

My Friend 'Toby'

Written on the death of my wee pet dog.

When Autumn leaves were falling,
I lost my dearest friend,
My faithful little "Toby" –
A true friend tae the end.

We roamed the fields together,
When Summer days were fine,
My orders he did obey,
He was a true friend of mine.

A playmate of the children,
He loved them everyone,
As they played around the doorway,
He joined in with the fun.

And he was ever watchful,
When danger came their way,
And with their little bits of scraps,
They fed him day by day.

He had no class or pedigree,
But just the common kind,
He was the best of company –
A good record left behind.

He's gone: I'll sadly miss him:
My loss I do regret;
But still I'll keep in memory,
My faithful little pet.

My Dog – My Friend to The End[15]

The best friend a man has in this world may turn against him, and become his enemy. His son or daughter that he has reared with loving care may prove ungrateful. Those who are nearest and dearest to us, those whom we trust with our happiness and good name, may become traitors to their faith. The money that a man has he may lose. It flies away from him, perhaps when he needs it most. A man's reputation may be sacrificed in a moment of ill-considered action. The people who are prone to fall on their knees to do us honour when success is with us, may be first to throw the stone of malice when failure settles its cloud upon our heads.

The one absolute friend that a man can have in this world, the one that never deserts him, the one that never proves ungrateful or treacherous, is his dog. A man's dog stands by him in prosperity and poverty, in health or sickness. He will sleep on the cold ground, when the wintry winds blow and the snow drives fiercely, if only by his master's side. He will try to soothe the wounds and sores that are encountered with

[15] Among Robert McLeod's papers was this recitation, 'My Dog – My Friend to The End'. Though there is no note of where he got it, or who wrote it, during the intervening years the piece has become famous as one of the most emotive speeches in the English language. It is attributed to a young, American lawyer from Missouri, George Graham Vest (1830–1904), whose debating skills earned him a place in the US Senate between 1879 and 1903. The speech, which he apparently repeated on hundreds of occasions, was written when he was representing a dog owner who was devastated that his neighbour shot his dog. He decided that the most effective way of convincing the jury was to focus on the theme of fidelity and thus appeal to the sentiment of the jury. He won the case.

As the previous page shows, McLeod was a dog-lover, and, like any owner, was saddened by the loss of his faithful little dog. Below is a transcription of the piece, with MacLeod's minimal changes that demonstrate his insight into what is termed as 'performance'– in order to deliver a convincing performance of any song or recitation, the performer, must be comfortable with the content. Within the 'folk idiom' it is common practice to change occasional words or phrases in order to personalise or give a more convincing delivery. MacLeod's changes are noted in brackets.

the roughness of the world. [The original has "He will kiss the hand that has no food to offer; he will lick the wounds and sores that come in an encounter with the roughness of the world."] He guards the sleep of his pauper master as if he were a prince. When all other friends desert him he remains. When riches take wings, and reputation falls to pieces, he is as constant in his love as the sun in its journey through the heavens.

If misfortune [fortune] drives his master forth as an outcast in the world, friendless and homeless, the faithful dog asks no higher privilege than that of accompanying him to guard him against dangers, against his enemies. And when the last scene of all comes, and death takes his master in its embrace and his body is laid away in the cold earth, no matter if all the friends pursue their way, there by the grave-side will his faithful dog be found, his watchfulness: a true friend even in death.

The Smile of a Child

The smile of a child, how pleasant to the sight;
A sweet little face and eyes shining bright,
The tender form of nature, so fair to see,
The smile of a child is heaven to me.

In her little cot where she goes to sleep,
While angels, silent, watch over her keep,
When in dreamland where she loves to be,
The smile of a child is heaven to me.

Then from her slumber she wakes with delight,
And jostles the clothes with her little might,
When in mother's arms she tosses with glee,
The smile of a child is heaven to me.

When sunbeams beacon to heighten her way,
As there on the floor with her toys at play,
When she falls asleep on Daddy's knee,
The smile of a child is heaven to me.

Tae a Robin

Ah! welcome tae ye Robin,
My wee red-breistit chum,
Again ye hae returned,
And lookin for a crumb,
But I hae plenty in my hoose,
Ye're welcome tae a share,
Although a simple miner bard,
I can work for plenty mair.
So come awaa my little freen,
Hop, hop upon the step,
For mony a sang tae me ye've sung
And that I'll ne'er forget,
When aa the hills were clad wi snaw,
The fields aa barren and bare,
I've lookit oot the doorway
Tae see if you were there.

And noo ye hae came back again,
A shelter here tae find,
I cannae see you suffer cauld,
Tae you I will be kind,
So Robin come awaa wi me,
I'll tak ye tae my shed
Wi a pickle hay just cut in May,
Ye'll get a warm bed.
I'll leave bye noo Red Robin,
The nicht is gathering fast,
The clouds are driving ower the hills,
There's gaun tae be a blast,
But noo I dinnae care for that
As lang's my wee freen's cosy,
The morn he'll sing a bonnie sang,
Wi his breistie bricht and rosy.

Into my humble cot I go,
The bairns come around me sobbin,
Looking so eager in my face
And asking whaur is Robin?
I tell them he has gone tae rest,
It pleases big and smaa,
They're glad that he is sheltered frae
The biting frost and snaw.
And noo they'll aa get cuddled down,
Into their bed though puir,
I've taught them in their childish way,
Tae say an evening prayer.
And when the dawn o morn comes,
I can see him there again
Sitting on the window-sill,
Tap, tapping on the pane.

The bairns love tae hear him sing,
It fills their herts wi glee,
Aa fed him wi the crumbs
That faa frae their daddie's knee;
They rin tae meet him at the door,
Where the golden sun shines in,
And there they play wi Robin
Till school hours they begin.
And when the dreary winter's past,
I heave a weary sigh
When tae my little feathered freend
I hae tae say good-bye,
When flowers lie dead in their snowy bed,
He's aye welcome back tae me.

Tae a Skylark

Sing on sweet songster to the glory of the day,
Thou has taught me to love in a tender way,
Singing to thy mate a sweet song of love,
Soaring on thy wing 'neath the blue sky above.

From the grey break of dawn till evening's setting sun,
To build thy downy nest thy task has begun,
Warbling so sweetly from yon mossy heap,
While daisies from their beds their little heads peep.

How lovely the fields of sweet-scented clover,
'Neath the bright summer sun thou loves tae hover,
Swinging to and fro in the fresh balmy air,
Away from all danger, sorrow and care.

Oh cruel be the hand thy nestie would rob,
To take away thy treasure how thy breistie would throb;
May this tender love from me never depart,
For oh, how I love the sweet song of the lark!

Songs

Pits and Politics

The Ghost Section, Number 2 Pit, Bowhill

I'm working in Number Twa pit,
In number five west run,
Beside a squad o' jolly boys,
And by jings they tak the bun.
It's known as the 'Ghost Section',
And they're never at a loss;
For they can depend upon the man,
And that's stripper, 'Andy Ross'.

CHORUS.
      They are the men, the hardy, hardy men,
      They dae their wark tae perfection,
      They dinna start tae blaw till they get a pint or twa:
      The boys that work in Number Five Ghost Section.

We hiv the great Trapper Gibson,
He is a sturdy chiel,
And collier Bob Spence, ye ken,
Wha keeps the run gey weel.
And then we've 'Sunshine Martin',
He daes aa that's in his power,
And no forgetting oor auld Leith man,
That's handsome Paddy Dewar.

There's Neber Wilson and Pat Cairns,
Oor steel men aye sae true:
And Bob Mills tae lead them on,
For he kens what they can do.
Their slogan is 'Safety First',
They aye like tae show their best:
It is their plan tae save a man
When puttin tae the test.

They work in the best o harmony,
That's their motto ane an aa.
There's mony a braw fitba match
Played up and doon the waa;
They roar oot, "That's a penalty kick!"
Withoot asking the referee.
But when they aa start shouting "Post!"
It pits the tin hat on me.

THE GHOST SECTION.

No. 2 Pit, Bowhill.

I'm working in number twa pit,
  In number five west run,
Beside a squad o' jolly boys,
  And by jings they tak' the bun.
It's known as the "Ghost Section,"
  And they're never at a loss ;
For they can depend upon the man,
  And that's stripper " Andy Ross."

CHORUS.

They are the men, the hardy, hardy men,
  They dae their wark up tae perfection,
They dinna start tae blaw till they get a pint or twa :
  The boys that work in number five Ghost Section.

We hiv the great " Trapper Gibson,"
  He is a sturdy chiel,
And collier " Bob Spence," ye ken,
  Wna keeps the run gey weel.
And then we've "Sunshine Martin,"
  He daes a' that's in his power :
And no forgetting oor auld Leith man,
  That's handsome " Paddy Dewar."

There's "Neber Wilson" and " Pat Cairns,"
  Oor steel men aye sae true :
And " Bob Mills " tae lead them on,
  For he kens what they can do.
Their slogan is Safety First,
  They aye like tae show their best :
It is their plan tae save a man
  When puttin' tae the test.

They work in the best o' harmony,
  That's their motto ane an' a'.
There's mony a braw fitba' match
  Played up and doon the wa' :
They roar oot that's a penalty kick
  Withoot asking the referee.
But when they a' start shouting post,
  It pits the tin hat on me.

ROBERT MacLEOD, Miner Poet.

I Want Tae See My Daddy

or 'The Dangers of the Mine.'

A miner bade his wife goodbye,
To toil in the depths below,
One little knows the danger
He has to undergo.
He left his boy, his only joy, in his cosy little bed,
The boy awoke from a dreadful dream,
To his mother then he said:

CHORUS
    "I want to see my daddy,
    I want to see my dad,
    But I know he will come back to me,"
    Said the miner's little lad,
    "I know he loves you mother,
    And to me he is very kind,
    O God protect my daddy,
    From the dangers of the mine."

The news of an explosion,
In the mine had taken place,
O sad were the cries of the little boy,
As he looked on his mother's face.
"I would like to save my daddy,"
He said with tearful eye,
"Although a boy and young in years,
I'm willing for a try."

CHORUS
    "I want tae see my daddy,
    I want tae see my dad,
    I prayed for him this morning,"
    Said the miner's little boy,

"And my mother she is waiting,
And to me is very kind,
O God protect my daddy,
From the dangers of the mine."

Then home at last, the danger past,
Alone he had been saved,
And when the boy he saw his dad,
How his little heart it braved,
He pressed his boy to his ragged breast,
And stroked his curly head,
One loving kiss, one fond embrace,
The boy again he said.

CHORUS
"Thank God I've seen my daddy,
Thank God I've seen my dad,
I prayed for you this morning,"
Said the miner's little lad
"Once again we are united,
For to me you're very kind,
Thank God he saved my daddy,
From the dangers of the mine."

Stop Yer Working Jock

To the Tune, 'Stop Yer Ticklin Jock.'

O I'm juist a simple collier cheil,
I've wrocht sixteen years in the pit,
But I hiv been idle the last eight weeks,
And I dinnae mean tae mak a hit,
For I got a place in a certain pit,
But the tonnage wis faur ower wee,
I wis juist about tae mak a start,
When my neighbour shouted oot tae me.

CHORUS
"Will ye stop yer working Jock,
O stop yer working Jock,
Dinnae work eleven shifts,
Ye're keeping up aa the folk
I wish you'd stop yer working,
Ye're filling up Methil Dock.
Stop yer working, Stop yer working,
Stop yer working Jock!

I tellt him then tae hurry up,
Says I, "Man, Tam, juist try yer best,
Ye ken we hae a lot o pay,
The tally book and aa the rest,"
But he says, "Man Jock hoo can I work,
Wi that air I'm like tae dee?"
He flung the graith intae the hutch,
And again he shouted oot tae me:

CHORUS

Noo they speak o big reductions
I think it's time we had a rise,
But the maisters are a gey hard lot,
And wi the miner they'll no sympathise,
So when ye're hail and healthy,
And making a steady wage,
Juist pit an extra shillin by,
Tae help ye along in yer auld age.

Love

Portobello Nellie

I'm in love wi a braw wee lassie,
A braw wee lassie is she,
I met her at the fair time,
By the side o the silvery sea,
When I looked at her, she looked at me,
Then I asked her tae be mine,
She looked sae shy, but said, "Och aye!",
Noo I'm singing aa the time.

CHORUS
> She's ma ain wee Portobello Nellie,
> Her other name's McLean,
> She's juist the lass wi plenty cash
> That I'm gaun tae caa my ain.
> I met her on the promenade
> By the side o the silver sea,
> I'm the fellow that's gaun tae marry Nellie,
> And Nellie's gaun tae marry me.

Her cheeks they are like roses,
Her hair as black as jet,
Aa day lang in her ear I sang
"Ye'll be ma darling pet!"
Oor style was fascinating
Tae the croods as they passed by,
When I stole a kiss,
She looked like this,
And I couldna help but cry.

CHORUS

Noo, her faither and her mither
They like me awfu weel,
I wonder if they'll be the same,
When Nellie's heart I steal;
And when oor weddin nicht comes roon,
I'm gaun tae dance the Hieland Fling,
And if I'm asked tae sing a sang,
This is the song I'll sing:

CHORUS

Ugly Mary o Argyle[16]

I have heard the kettle singin,
The tea-pat on the hob,
I hae seen the chairs gang flingin,
When I couldna get a job.
And her false face, it has feared me,
In the morning when she rose,
I thocht it time tae hook it:
'Twas far better, I suppose.

Through the hoose the cups gaed fleein,
By jings she went her mile!
And I wish I ne'er had mairrit,
Ugly Mary o Argyle,
Wi a voice like roarin thunder,
And her een red, white and blue,
She said she'd tear me asunder,
Or the mangle me puit through.

Still tae me she has been dearer,
Wi the debt she's taken on,
My very Sunday troosers,
Are lying in the pawn.
Noo I wish she'd kick the bucket,
Then I wad wear my tyle,
And I'd say ta-ta for ever,
Tae ugly Mary o Argyle.

---

[16] In MacLeod's day, the song 'Bonnie Mary o Argyle' had become an all-time concert favourite, recorded on 78 rpm discs by many popular singers, such as John McCormack (1914) and Heddle Nash (1931). The original lyrics were composed around 1850 by Charles Jeffrey who was inspired by the story of Robert Burns and his 'Highland Mary'. Jeffrey then collaborated with fellow Englishman S. Nelson who composed the melody.

Label of the 78 rpm disc of Mary of Argyle sung by
Sir Harry Lauder

The Bonnie Lass o Letham Glen

There's a bonnie, bonnie lassie,
Doon in the Letham Glen,
She's just the nicest lass
O aa the yins I ken,
I've juist noo sent a letter
Tae my joy and heart's delight,
That I'm coming on my holidays
When the sun is shining bright.

CHORUS
Tae my bonnie, bonnie lassie
O the bonnie Letham Glen,
Wi lips as red as roses,
I caa her my lovely Jen,
It's her I'll be treatin,
So I'm longing for the meetin,
Wi my bonnie, bonnie lassie,
Awaa doon in Letham Glen.

When I see my bonnie dear
I'm gaun tae tell you this:[17]
I'll fling my airms roon her neck,
On her cheek I'll plant a kiss,
And I ken a fine wee hoosie
Wi a cosy but-an-ben,
It's there we'll live in happiness
In a spot near Letham Glen.

---

[17] Line missing; this is a suggested replacement.

The Factory Lass

I'm a decent factory lass,
My name is Kate McKie,
I ken I'm guid-looking,
Although I look kind o shy,
I've courted some lads in my time,
Yes, alloo me tae remark,
But the yin I'm coortin noo,
He's gey often in the dark,

CHORUS
My lad's a braw lad, a braw lad is he,
I'm awfu fond o him, and he's awfu fond o me,
He kisses me and cuddles me, I think it jolly fine,
And I'm wearying for the day that I'll be his,
and he'll be mine.

The first place I met him,
It wis at the July Fair,
He says, "My bonnie lassie,
Ye have awfu bonnie hair."
The way he treated me that day,
I'm shair I'll ne'er forget,
He caaed me his sugar-doddle-um,
And little darlin pet.

CHORUS

Noo he's promised for tae marry me
In a month or so,
I'll juist wait till that time,
And it will be domino,
I'll teach him hoo tae keep the hoose,
I'll be free o care and strife,
What a happy lass I will be,
When I become his little wife!

Jessie The Flouer o Dunblane[18]

The moon had gone doon roon the back o the coal hoose,
The fish shops had shut before we gaed hame;
Just then I met a lassie, oh my, she was classie!
And it happened tae be Jessie the flouer o Dunblane.
She'd a hump on her back like a big water melon,
Ye wad thocht her hair had ne'er seen a kame;
She puff-poothers her face wi a dab o Cherry Blossom,
And she caas hersel 'Jessie the flouer o Dunblane'.

FIRST CHORUS
     Is the grate-polish faced Jessie, is Monkey Brand[19] Jessie,
     Is towsy-haired Jessie, the flouer o Dunblane?

Her buits are as big as the boats at the Ferry,
At dancin a fox-trot, oh mind she's a don;
When she gangs through the hall, the flair gangs a-creakin,
She disnae care about dancin without her big crushers on.
She's learnin the eightsome, tae dance wi a kiltie,
She swings to and fro like a ship in distress,
And when she starts waltzin, ye've tae steer for the doorway
Tae mak room for this damsel they caa flet-fitted Jess.

SECOND CHORUS
     Is this dancin Jessie, is this prancin Jessie
     Is this glancin Jessie, the flouer o Dunblane?

She aince got the jile for robbin a grave-yaird,
She taen the doos aff the tombstones tae gie them a flee;
She lifted her tools frae the strawberry pickin,
But was apprehended sellin chewing-gum on the road tae Dundee.

---

[18] A parody of "Jessie the Flower o Dunblane" by Robert Tannahill (1774–1810), which begins "The sun has gane down o'er the lofty Ben Lomond".

[19] Monkey Brand soap was a scouring soap that was produced in 1899, advertised to clean any surface but 'it won't wash clothes'.

When she asked me tae marry, I cried, "Oh Dear, murder!
Gie me a sleepin-poother, tae put mysel ootae pain!"
I wad rather tease oakum for a year and a twelve month,
Than marry this flapper, the flouer o Dunblane.

THIRD CHORUS
     This sooty-faced Jessie, tooty-fruity moothed Jessie,
     This harum-scarum Jessie, the flouer o Dunblane.

Lay My Head Beneath A Rose

Possibly to the tune of 'She was poor but she was honest'
by music-hall entertainer Billy Bennett, (1887–1942.)

Darling, fling me frae yer bosom,
As ye did the nicht before,
When ye nearly knocked me speechless,
At oor ain wee kitchen door,
Ye were kind and very gentle,
Wi an axe ye split my nose,
In the morning I lay moaning:
Lay my head beneath a rose.

CHORUS
Lay me where the bells are ringing,
Where the beer and whisky flows,
When it's time for chucking out, love,
Lay my head beneath a rose.

Darling, first when we got marrit,
You did promise tae obey,
But you've turned oot a tartar,
And noo I rue that awfu day,
Lay me quietly doon tae rest dear,
Where the tombstones stand in rows,
When I hear a horn blawing,
I'll be curling up my toes.

CHORUS

When I reach the golden shore, love,
I'll send you a nice P.C.
It will be a polis in disguise, love,
For the way you have treated me.
And if ye chance tae marry anither,
May yer joys aa come tae woes,
Tis then you will remember me, love,
Lying safe beneath a rose.

Maggie Dobie

Parody on 'Johnnie Scobie.'[20]

As I went ower Benarty Hill,
Tae look for a bit jobbie,
'Twas there I met a bonnie lass,
And they caaed her Maggie Dobie.
Says I, my lass, whaur are ye gaun?
For poetry is my hobby,
And a verse or twaa I'll write for you,
If you be Maggie Dobie.

CHORUS

I'm no awaa tae bide awaa,
I'm no awaa tae leave ye,
I'm no awaa tae bide awaa,
I'll aye come back and see ye.

I told the lass I loued her weel,
Juist as I loued ma toddy,
She flung her airms aroon my neck,
Saying "I love Johnnie Scobie."
We taen a walk aroon the hill,
The nicht was getting foggy,
We wandered on a mile or twaa,
For she loved Johnnie Scobie.

CHORUS

---

[20] Among MacLeod's papers were two versions of this song. The other one has
Peeweep in the first line, instead of Benarty.

We had a rest that hour was best,
'Twas there I met ma bogey,
Wi a tear in her ee she then asked me,
If I'd mak her Mrs. Scobie?
I taen her hame that very nicht,
And seen her in the lobby
We kissed and vowed that we'd get wed,
So she'd be Mrs. Scobie.

Community and Family

Bella in the Bath

Tune: 'Stop Yer Ticklin Jock'

Oh, I'm marrit tae a sonsie wife;
Mind ye, she's a teaser, oh!
Sixteen stane o flesh and bane:
I've tae dae a lot tae please her, oh.
When she rises in the morning,
On me she'll shower her wrath:
"Noo hurry, John, get yer trousers on,
For ye hiv tae wash me in the bath."

CHORUS
    Will ye stop yer ticklin, John!
    Oh stop yer ticklin John,
    The folk will hear ye doon below,
    The way ye're carryin on,
    I wish ye'd stop yer ticklin,
    And dinnae mak me laugh,
    But wash me bonnie, my wee John,
    And mind I'm in the bath.

Intae the bathroom there she goes,
Then turns the watter on,
She climbs intae the bathtub
Sic a sicht tae look upon,
Noo canny wi yer Bella, John,
For ye ken the tender place;
My cheeks they turn a rosy red,
When I saw her navel base.

Noo John, gang roond my hippodrome;
Yes, mak yer Bella clean and braw,
And when it comes up tae my toes,
Mak them white as driven snaw,
And dinnae ye get fidgey, John,
But keep on the richt path
For when Adam christened Eve,
He did it gentle in the bath.

Bonnie Bella Broon[21]

Tune: 'Wee Nellie M'Kie'

I'm a car conductress,
My name is Bella Broon,
Aa the lads they smile at me
As I gang hurlin through the toon,
I like the job aa richt, ye ken,
Though at times I'm rather shy,
And I pad up and doon the stair
And the laddies they dae cry.

CHORUS
Oh! there's bonnie wee Bella,
Bonnie wee Bella Broon,
Juist the sort o lassie
I would like tae spoon!
And when they start tae tease me,
I juist look up tae the stars;
They aa want tae love this little dove
The conductress on the cars.

My route is frae Dunfermline
Tae Cowdenbeath and tae Lochore;
The boys keep singin in my ear,
"Tis Bella, we adore!"
When I see the passengers seated
I blow my whistle or tinkle the bell,
Oh! it's nice when ye get civility
Frae the collier and the swell.

---

[21] This page was among MacLeod's original papers, dated 1924.

Inverkeithing Brass Band

Tune: 'I Like Tae Follow The Band'

Oh, hiv ye seen oor ain Brass Band?
Dae they no look braw?
Tae see them marchin doon the street,
They're a credit tae us aa,
I'm awfu fond o music,
It is a charming thing,
When they turn oot, ye hear me shout,
And this is what I sing:

CHORUS
As I walk doon the street,
I think it juist a treat,
Tae listen tae them play;
We were aince faur back in Inverkeithing,
But we're no faur back the day.
When G. Forrester is in command
He'll train them up tae win a cup,
The Inverkeithing Brass Band.

Noo, wi patience and perseverance,
And each yin doing their best –
The Basses and Trombones, the Euphonium and Horns
The Cornets and aa the rest,
And when in a competition,
We hope tae tak oor stand,
We'll cry hooray when they win the day –
The Inverkeithing Brass Band.

I'll Gang Roon Wi The Hat

Though no tune was suggested, the song fits the tune 'Bonnie
Wee Jeannie McColl'

A gang o chaps, including me, had naethin else tae do,
We thocht upon a caper tae raise a bob or two,
So we held a general meetin in a close, ye understand,
And came tae the conclusion we wad start a German Band.

CHORUS
    I'll gang roon wi the hat, my boys,
    I'll gang roon wi the hat,
    I'll tak care o the chink, chink, chink,
    I'm awfu guid at that,
    I'll gang roon wi the bouncey bounce,
    As lively as a cat,
    I'll be the heid cashier o the band,
    So I'll gang roon wi the hat.

This German Band turned oot a frost, we couldna mak oor meat,
Although we made an awfu noise in every blessed street,
The hale o us were hungry, and fu o discontent,
So I proposed that every chap should pawn his instrument.

CHORUS

We made oor first appearance in a quiet-looking street,
But we had tae keep oor eyes upon the bobbies on the beat,
We sang a dizzen sangs an mair, surrounded by a crowd o weans,
But though we did oor level best, got sweet naethin for oor pains.[22]

CHORUS

---

[22] As the syllables may be awkward to sing, this line could be rendered as 'But
though we did oor level best, got naethin for oor pains.'

I'll Never Gang Back Tae Leslie

My name's Geordie Neil, a chap ye ken weel;
Ye'll aa see I'm a little bit hamely,
My brithers are fair, but the lassies declare
That I'm the flouer o the faimily,
When I gang oot tae walk aboot
I'm fairly confounded,
In less than a thrice its awful nice
Wi lassies tae be surrounded.

CHORUS
O the lassies start tae gash me[23]
Every time they pass me;
They tug my hair till I roar "It's sair!"
So I'll never gae back tae Leslie.

Wan nicht tae a ball I gaed tae the hall
Tae jine wi them in a Lancers,
When a fellow did roar
"Leave yer feet at the door,
If ye mean tae be yin o the dancers!"
We reeled and squealed and jumped and thumped
And then there wis a shindy;
They emptied the hall efter the ball,
And then flung me ower the windy.

The lassies crooded aroon oor door
Each nicht like the merriest boozers,
And I hiv tae shout, "I cannae come oot
For my mither's mendin my troosers,"
The lassies crooded aroon oor door,
There's naebody here tae chase ye;
As shair as daith, the claes are claith
We only want tae embrace ye.

---

[23] Though the manuscript copy has 'gas', it is more likely that MacLeod would have used the Scots word 'gash' ('chat up', gossip, prattle loudly).

My Ain Wee Hoose

Tune: 'My Ain Wee Hoose'

There's wee bit humble placie,
They caa Barlinnie Jile,
Whaur they feed ye on cauld parritch,
And a drink o caster ile.

CHORUS
In yer ain wee cell
Aye, ye're by yersel,
O there's nae place in the warld,
Like yer ain wee cell,
Like yer ain wee cell.

Ye get skirlie[24] for yer dinner,
Made wi a single pea,
And if ye dinnae tak it,
Ye can either live or dee.

There's a warder staunin ready,
And if ye chance tae speak,
He'll cleave ye wi his baton,
And send you fast asleep.

Ye gang tae kirk on Sunday,
And sit aa in a raw,
And when the sermon's ended,
Wan by wan ye're marched awaa.

---

[24] The manuscript had 'skeely'.

My Little Yo-yo

Possible tune: 'The Week efter the Fair' or 'The Hail Week
o the Fair'.

Oh what is this we're getting noo?
It's the craze o aa the toon,
This game they caa the yo-yo,
And ye bob it up an doon.
Aa the ladies in oor street,
They're yellin oot hullo!
The very cats in oor back green,
They're playing at yo-yo.

CHORUS

Wad ye like tae have a go-go,
On my little yo-yo?
Aa the ladies say it's something grand,
I'm walkin doon the street,
They say I'm juist a treat,
Wi my little yo-yo in my hand.
I come from Skye and sing "Hooch Aye!"
I belong tae a happy little band,
Wi my little yo-yo in my hand.

Last Saturday at the dancing
A lassie said tae me,
"Can yer yo-yo bob-bob?
For I would like tae see,"
Says I, "My dear, ye're awfu queer,
Have ye got me on a string?"
I flung my arms roon her neck,
And then began tae sing.

CHORUS

I took a walk into the zoo,
Juist tae see the show,
The monkeys aa sat in a row,
Playing at yo-yo,
And Jumbo the elephant
Went marching roon the ring.
When he started playing yo-yo,
We aa began tae sing.

CHORUS

Oor Jock's Learned Tae Dance

Tune: Original.[25]

Hiv ye heard o my big brither Jock?
He's nearly gone insane.
Since he went tae the dance hall
He's got dancin on the brain.
He'll drag me oot o my bed at nicht,
He dreams I'm the M.C.
He kicks the cat below the bed,
And cries oot this tae me:

CHORUS
    Oh put the partners right and left,
    Then swing four.
    Turn the ladies on the right,
    You should hear him roar.
    Roond the kitchen table
    He does fairly prance;
    Oor Jock is nearly crazy,
    Since he learned hoo tae dance.

He's a devil for a wee "Fox Trot",
Or a guid auld "Scotch Reel",
And when he does the "Charleston",
You ought tae hear him squeal,
He comes hame whistling "The Twilight Waltz",
For the jiggin he does adore;
When mither cries him for his wark,
Tis then he starts tae roar.

---

[25] So far (2015) I have not found an original tune, although the song could be sung to the tune of "Phil the Fluter's Ball" by Percy French (1854–1920), the Irish entertainer and song-writer who was very popular in MacLeod's day.

Simple Peter Pimple

I'm Simple Peter Pimple, I'm a duffer, so they say,
But tak my tip, I'm no as green's I look.
I cannae say my lessons, and I'm punished every day,
For makkin pipe lichts wi my copy book.
My hert's fairly sick o that thing caaed arithmetic,
Grammar pits me in an awfu state,
So I listen for the bell, and wait –[26]
Tis the only thing for me, it suits me tae a T.

CHORUS

    Puir wee Peter Pimple looks sae awfu simple,
    Little Peter Pimple's no a fuil,
    He's silly and he's daft,
    But he's the champion ignoramus o the schuil.

The master aften tells me I've naething in my heid,
But my mither kens that when she cambs my hair.
It's a very funny thing, I cannae learn tae read or write,
They say that I'm as stubborn as a bear.
Theology and geometry and likewise rhyme and prose,
It's enough tae drive a lad like me insane,
And before I wad say my lessons I'd gae hungry tae my bed,
Or stand a hundred palmies wi the cane.

---

[26] Line missing; this is a suggested replacement.

Tamson's Fancy Ball[27]

Ye'll see by my appearance I'm as jolly as can be,
I'm juist noo frae a fancy ball, it wis a glorious spree,
There wis a crood and nae mistake that nicht inside the hall,
There were her and me, and me and she, at Tamson's fancy ball.

CHORUS
    When I came in as the Duke o Argyle
    I began tae out it pat,
    Knocked ower the boys wi my corduroys
    and Sunday-Monday hat,
    My lass was there and she looked fair,
    as along the flair we tore,
    Mary M'Gall taen the Belle o the Ball
    and I taen the bell o the door.

The Sisters McNab were there that nicht, wi ruffles roun their throats,
Big Jean McCraw looked jist as braw as Mary Queen o Scots,
The Prince o Wales wis Tam Mckie, but I am glad tae tell,
The yin that fairly taen the cake, I think it wis masel.

CHORUS

Of coorse we had a supper, we had a lot tae drink and eat,
Everything and onything, exceptin lots o meat,
But when I asked Tamson for a drink, forget I never shall,
He taen me oot tae the tap o the stair, and pinted tae the waal.[28]

---

[27] The song is reminiscent of other comic songs, such as the 'Hielandman's Fancy Ball'. Though no tune is suggested, it could also be sung to the Gaelic song,'Brochan Lom', which has long been part of the accordion repertoire . The catchy rhythm of the fourth line, 'There were her and me, and me and she, at Tamson's fancy ball' fits perfectly.

[28] He pointed to the well.

The Lochgelly Pipe Band

Tune: 'When Tommy Comes Home Again.'[29]

On the first day o May, that is the day
Oor pipe band will turn out;
When we see them in their kilts sae braw
We'll gie them a hearty shout.
As they parade oor streets aa roon,
We'll cry hip, hip hooray!
For oor gallant chums wi pipes and drums,
And this is what we'll say.

CHORUS
> Wi a rum-tum-tooral-um
> Wi a rum-tum-tay,
> The ladies will be singin,
> And the lassies they'll be gay,
> The folks will enjoy themsels
> As they tak their stand,
> And listen tae the music
> O oor ain pipe band.

Some o the boys hiv duin their bit,
Ye will agree wi me,
So let us gie them a welcome,
Wi herts sae gay and free,
We'll turn oot, baith big and smaa,
And hae a jolly time,
Gie them a shake for freenship sake,
And days o auld lang syne.

---

[29] Composed by English music-hall entertainer, Lawrence Barclay (1898–1949).

THE LOCHGELLY PUBLIC PIPE BAND 1906
BACK ROW: Pipe Major G. Marshall;, A. Cochrane, J. Smith, A. Reid, G. Swan & A. Greig.
FRONT ROW: J. Smith, M. Easson, F. Jackson, J. Erskine & T. Graham.

The Merry Lads Dancing

Tune: 'I'm Happy Wi Ma Chappie'

Are ye gaun tae the dancin?
It is a grand affair,
Me and my chum we mak things hum,
So I hope tae see ye there.
When ye come into oor town hall
Where there is fun galore,
And the lassies they are happy
And the laddies they do roar.

CHORUS
    I'll treat ye tae a Fox Trot,
    A Two-Step or a Waltz,
    If you refuse, I'll be in the Blues,
    Or say my feet are false
    There's Isa, Jean, and Nellie,
    Wee Aggie, Kate, and Belle,
    They can trip the light fantastic
    Wi the collier or the swell.

The music it is guid, I'm shair,
As played by Baxter's Band,
And oor M.C., good old R.P.,
 He'll be there in command,
So juist you say the word, ye ken,
And along the flair we'll prance,
For if ye like a guid nicht oot[30]
I'll meet ye at the dance.

---

[30] Missing line; suggested replacement.

The Sugar-Doddle Shop[31]

My name is Rab McDougal,
I keep a sugar-doddle shop
And customers aboot the place,
Oot and in they pop,
They like ma sugar-doddle,
They say it's something grand,
And march aff tae the kirk on Sunday,
Wi a lump o it in their haun.

CHORUS
Jock likes his doddle, Jean likes her doddle,
They sook it an never think tae stop;
They tak it in their hand, and say it's something grand,
A lump o sugar-doddle oot ma sugar-doddle shop.

Noo at the Kirk last Sunday
When the plate wis handed round,
Auld Annie White searched for her mite,
But no trace o it was found,
She then got in an awfu fuss,
As the collector he came near,
But she took him by the tail-coat
And whispered in his ear.

CHORUS

Auld Maggie Broon came in last nicht,
And she said, "Noo look here Rab,
They say yer doddle's awfu guid,
O it I'd like a dab,"
Says I, "Maggie dear, come ben the room,
It's juist noo aff the fire,
And if ye've time tae wait a while
Ye'll get as much as ye require."

---

[31] Sugar-doddle is an old fashioned candy.

Tribute Tae Bowhill & District Prize Pipe Band

On their success 1930. Tune: 'When the Boys Come Home
Again.'[32]

O, hiv ye seen oor famous band,
Aye, dae they no look braw?
Tae see them wi their kilts and plaids,
They're a credit tae us aa,
They've proved their worth in piping,
And won laurels tae their name;
Hoo prood we feel, we wish them weel,
Oor ain Pipe Band o fame.

CHORUS
As they walk doon the street, it's just a treat,
Tae listen tae them play,
At "Lammas Fair", I dae declare,
They won the trophy richt away,
At March, Strathspey, and guid Scotch reel,
They were something grand,
Tae oor hert's content, the cup it went
Tae the Bowhill Prize Pipe Band.

In mony a contest they hiv been,
And each did their best,
Oor gallant chums, wi pipes and drums,
The committee and aa the rest,
All honour tae Pipe Major Herd,
As there he took his stand;
He trained them up and they won the cups,
The Bowhill Prize Pipe Band.

CHORUS

---

[32] Composed by E. W. Rogers, who also wrote the lyrics of the original.

BOWHILL & DISTRICT PIPE BAND

The Coronation Day

Tune: 'We all went Marching Home'

The Coronation of our Queen,
It was a great event
All the lords and ladies
Your humble servant they had sent.
So I went away to London town
To see the sights so gay
And this little chorus I did sing
Before I went away.

CHORUS
Come along with me now
And join the grand array:
Come along and sing a song
And be ready for the fray.
All the children in our town
They shouted out "Hooray!"
And sang aloud "God Save the Queen"
On the Coronation Day.

When Her Majesty came on the scene
There was an awful crush:
The Navy, Army and Air Force
They could avoid the rush,
And as we marched along the Mall
The bands did gaily play:
We sang "Long live Her Majesty"
On the Coronation Day.

Football and Sport

Willie Pullar wi the Little Twinklin Feet[33]

Tune: 'Barney Google.'[34]

You've heard o Willie Pullar,
Who's a dandy on the ba',
A clever little forward,
Jist as guid as ever ye saw,
He's aye upon the trot, ye ken,
As he prances doon the wing,
He is the idol o' the crood,
And this is what they sing.

CHORUS:
Willie Pullar wi' the little twinklin feet,
Willie Pullar, his play is jist a treat,
He slips the halfback and the back
Then at goal he has a whack
Willie Pullar wi the little twinklin feet.

When he gets on the baa I'm shair
It's grand to watch him play
For his size, he's a big surprise,
He's a marvel o the day.
His crosses they are aa weel-timed,
They suit Devlin, dae ye see,
And they come from artful Willie
O the Cowdenbeath F.C.

---

[33] Dated 1925.

[34] The melody was by Broadway music-hall composer, Con Conrad (1891–1938), who was probably best known for 'Ma, He's Making Eyes at Me'. The song (with lyrics by Billy Rose) can be heard on a 78 rpm recording (1923), available via the Library of Congress National Jukebox, <www.loc.gov/jukebox/recordings/detail/id/9316 >

David Allen of Cowdenbeath F.C. adds the following note:

Willie Pullar learned the arts of football whilst serving in the trenches in the 1st World War. He came to Cowdenbeath from Dalkeith Thistle in December 1921 and was a fixture at outside-right for 9 years at Central Park. Willie displayed his wonderful wing trickery in 294 League games for 'the Miners' - a Cowdenbeath appearance record that stood until the 1980's. Pullar's wizardry made him tremendously popular with the fans. He was another Cowdenbeath player who was on the verge of international recognition, being named as a reserve when Scotland played Wales in 1927... In 1930, Willie Pullar moved on to play for Leith Athletic and Leith enjoyed the spectacle of his wing play for a few seasons. A brief spell with Raith Rovers followed before the *'little twinklin feet'* twinkled no more.

Cowden's Famous Five[35]

You've heard o Cowden's famous five,
Their names are spreading wide,
At this awfu fitbaa game
They fairly tak a pride,
They've met and beat the best, ye ken,
They chase the leather weel,
They are the type tae do or die,
When they trip upon the field.

CHORUS
There's good old Joe MacDonald,
And sturdy Tommy Frame,
Wee Pullar wi the twinklin feet,
He'll no let the baa alane,
And Duncan Lindsay on the dot,
At goal he has a drive,
And hard working Michael Connaboy,
Make up Cowden's famous five.

Then here's good luck tae the boys in blue,
Lang may they toe the mark,
The boys that aa can play the game,
Frae guid auld Central Park,
They aa ken yin anither's play,
As doon the field they glide,
May they win prizes in galore,
Cowden's famous five-a-side.

---

[35] No tune is suggested, though several popular songs would fit. (e.g., Phil the Fluter's Ball)

The Fitba Referee

Of aa the men ye read aboot,
I'm shair ye'll aa agree,
There's nane sae muckle thocht o
As a fitbaa referee,
Wi a bobby's whistle in his mooth,
He rins aboot the park,
A when he's asked tae gie a goal,
He'll say it's juist a lark.

PATTER

Yon wis a match I can tell ye. Ye see, the fact wis I kent
naething aboot fitbaa at aa, it wis the money I wis efter,
and mony a time I've rued rinnin efter yon money. It
wis a faur waur business than the case o matrimony. But
when I got the P.C. stating I wis tae referee the match, a
split new suit o knickerbockers and a bobby's whustle,
awaa I went as innocent as a lamb tae be slaughtered,
and so I wis, but there will be green snow and red rain
when ye hear me shout again.

CHORUS

In me ye see a referee,
At least I yince wis wan,
And on the field did deftly wield,
Ma whussel like a man,
But friens, dear friens, believe you me,
Ma first match wis ma last,
For I cannae sit doon noo, my friens,
Tho years hae long gane past.

Ye've heard o Bruce at Bannockburn,
And Nelson's bravery,
But still, my friens, I will maintain,
They're no as brave as me,
For they had men tae back them up,
But I stood there mysel,
Wan man against a thousand,
Like this, my friends,[shaking] don't tell. [Shaking]

CHORUS

Cowdenbeath Versus Dunfermline

Tune: 'My Life's an Awfu Life'

At the meeting o oor rivals
It will cause an awfu steer,
We'll no forget the games they played,
When they finished up last year:
Dunfermline won the Qualifying Cup,
They fairly did the trick,
But they'll find they hiv enough tae dae
When they've Cowdenbeath tae lick.

CHORUS
    Guid luck tae auld Dunfermline,
    Likewise Cowdenbeath Royal Blue,
    We cannae forget the tussles they've had,
    And the games they hiv pulled through,
    Noo when they trip upon the field,
    And the game it does begin,
    We'll cry, "Hurry up and play the baa!
    And let the best team win."

Dunfermline ye'll aa admit wi me,
They are a sturdy lot,
But the victories o the Cowden boys
Can never be forgot,
They proved themselves in mony a match,
In days lang, lang gaun bye,
And when they face each other
We'll no forget tae cry:

CHORUS

What ever team does win the tie,
We'll praise them far and near,
We'll gie them aa the support we can,
So they dinnae need tae fear,
Wi the rattle o our crawmills,
Abune the din and strife,
We'll gie them aa a herty shake
If they keep the Cup in Fife.

Come Ye By Athol

Come ye by train, oh ye wi the funny feet,
Watch and no tumble or you'll rue it sairly,
Pu up yer knickers and draw doon yer jersey,
That's what they cry efter bandy-leg't Charlie.

CHORUS
Follow me, follow me, the ladies aa follow me,
Roond the goal-nets they aa bother me sairly,
Charlie, Charlie, wha widnae follow thee,
King o the goalies, three-cornered faced Charlie?

Whit maks them cry oot, "King o turf-lifters!"
I'm nae goalkeeper, that's honest and fairly,
Still, when I kick a baa, aa the wee deevils caa,
"Awaa pawn yer buits noo, big baa-heided Charlie."

We hiv a richt back, a gallant defender,
When he misses his kick he puts blame on me shairly,
When the baa's in the net he'll turn roon an tell me,
"Ye couldna catch the cauld, wire-nettin faced Charlie."

Footballers Take Care

Tune: 'Asleep in the Deep.'[36]

Stormy the day when the teams line up,
Tae play in the great cup tie,
The tussle begins, they cry "Watch yer shins!"
While others cry "That's ower shy!"
Now Wullie, jist watch this corner kick,
"Come on, noo, boy, an dae the trick!"
He's din it before, he's the boy tae score,
If we lose today we'll play fitbaa nae mair.

CHORUS
Loudly the crowd in the grandstand cheers,
While supporters are aa sheddin tears,
Half-backs beware, full-backs tak care,
The centre is near ye, beware, beware!
Beware, beware!
Mony a goalie gets rowed in a sheet,
So beware, beware!

Whit o the crood when the game is ower?
Whit of the puir referee?
Mony a nicht he sits up in bed,
Nursin a big black ee,
When aa the players come toddling hame,
They've had a dram at the end o the game,
O whit a sicht, they bid guid nicht,
Next time we meet them we'll beat them aa richt.

[36] The melody of this early 20th century song gives an insight into MacLeod's eclectic taste as well as his capability as a singer. Composed by H.W Petrie, the song has a big range and is vocally demanding, particularly for an untrained singer. MacLeod also parodies the original lyrics, which begin "Stormy the night..." The copy that survived among MacLeod's papers omits the repeat of 'Beware' in the chorus and in both verses, line 7 is missing. The repeats are written in full here, and replacements which fit the melody are suggested for the missing lines.

In D, (d to b)   In F, (f to d)   In G, (g to e)   In Bb, (bb to g)

In Eb   Duet   In Bb

Soprano or
Tenor (eb to ab)
and
Contralto or
Bass (eb to e)
(Melody Alternates)

Soprano or
Tenor (bb to g)
and
Alto or
Bass (bb to eb)
(Melody Alternates)

ASLEEP IN THE DEEP

SONG

LYRIC BY

ARTHUR J. LAMB

MUSIC BY

H. W. PETRIE

Solo 50¢ T   Duet 65¢ T

QUARTET — MALE, FEMALE AND MIXED VOICES 15 CENTS EACH NET

VIOLIN AND PIANO 50¢ T
CELLO AND PIANO 50¢ T

VIOLIN, CELLO
AND PIANO ___ 65¢ T

TRADEMARK   REGISTERED

STANDARD

M. WITMARK & SONS
NEW YORK

PRINTED IN U.S.A.

Guid Auld Davie Stevenson

Tune: 'Juist Being at Hame.'

We hae a dandy goalkeeper,
Davie Stevenson is his name;
He has been tried and tested,
At this awfu fitbaa game
He's aye upon the spot, ye ken,
As he stands between the sticks;
For the centre, half back and the backs,
He's up tae aa their tricks.

Guid auld Steve, yer goal ye dinnae leave,
But ye stop them on the line;
And as ye tip them ower the bar,
Yer judgement it is fine.
Lang may ye wear the colours true,
And in guid form be,
So guid luck tae Davie Stevenson,
O the Cowdenbeath F.C.

In mony a scrimmage ye hae been,
And come oot wi colours bright,
And saved the goal when aa seemed lost,
Tae the Cowden boys' delight,
We hope ye'll keep yer sheet aye clean,
Ye please us tae a T,
So we'll depend on good auld Stevie,
O the Cowdenbeath FC.

The Dundonald Bluebell F.C.

Winners of the Scottish Juveniles Cup 2nd. June 1946.
Tune: 'Oor ain Wee Fitba Club.'

There's a fit-baa team in Fife the noo,
It's the shining light too,
Ye'll ken the boys I mean,
That don the blue and white,
Ye'll aa admit wi me, I'm shair,
Our team they hiv dune weel;
Tae see them bring hame the cup,
Hoo prood we aa dae feel.

CHORUS
Then good luck tae the good old Bluebell,
We're glad they won the day,
And may they succeed in scoring goals,
In every match they play
Their supporters follow on,
They pleased them tae a T,
They've won the cup and we'll follow up,
Dundonald Bluebell F.C.

There's Adams in atween the sticks,
He's the boy that can fairly clear,
Wi Beath and Chalmers on the backs,
In them there is nae fear,
And what a grand half-back trio,
When puttin tae the test,
In Clark, Gavin and Neilson,
We hiv three halves o the best.

CHORUS

And noo we come tae the forward line,
They are a dashing lot,
For men like Strachan and Ormiston,
They're aye upon the dot,
And McIntyre in the centre,
He's a trier, ye can bet,
He's no content until the baa,
Is lying cosy in the net.

CHORUS

At last we come tae oor left-wing,
They are a clever pair –
Weatherspoon and Alexander,
None with them compare,
Not forgetting the Secretary,
And hard-working Committee,
We'll cry Hooray, they won the day!
Dundonald Bluebell F. C.

CHORUS

The Flying Fifer o The Glesga Rangers F.C.

Tune: 'Sandy Ye're a Dandy.'

There's a player wha fairly taks the ee
A guid yin noo ye'll aa agree,
On the baa he's a treat tae see
O Sandy, he's a dandy.
The wey that he can dance aboot,
And bang the baa wi either foot,
Nae wonder the spectators shout –
Sandy ye're a dandy!

CHORUS
    O Sandy ye're a dandy
    O Sandy ye're a don,
    Ye come in awfu handy
    As guid goals ye're pilin' on,
    Wi yer tricky little touches
    As guid as e'er we saw,
    We've outside richts in Scotland,
    But ye're the dandy o them aa.

Fifteen years ye've been at Rangers noo,
And donned the colours bonnie blue,
And aye ye proved sae staunch and true.
O Sandy ye're a dandy.
Tae see ye prancin doon the wing
And get the baa on the swing,
Mony a braw goal it does bring
O Sandy ye're a dandy.

The Raith Rovers F.C.

Tune: 'A Wee Doch an Doris.'

There's a team in bonnie Scotland,
A team sae staunch and true,
And that's old Raith Rovers
That wear the navy blue,
Ye'll aa admit wi me, I'm shair
They play awfu weel,
Tae see them bringing hame the cup
How prood we aa would feel.

CHORUS
   Here's luck tae good old Raith Rovers
   And may they win the day,
   And keep on scoring goals
   In every match they play.
   Their supporters they follow on,
   They please them tae a "T",
   We'll follow up the boys in blue,
   The good old Raith F.C.

There's Johnstone atween the posts,
The boy that can shairly clear;
McLure and McNaught on the backs,
In them there is nae fear,
And what a grand half-back trio
When they're put ye tae test;
In McLaughlin, Colville and Leigh,
We've three halfs o the best.

And noo we come tae the forward line,
They are a dashing lot;
For men like Maule and Young, ye ken,
They're aye upon the dot,
And Willie Penman in the centre,
He's a tricky lad ye bet;
He's no content until the baa,
Is lying cosy in the net.

At last we come tae the left-wing,
They're a clean and clever pair;
The combination o Murray and Brander,
Few wi them can compare,
And not forgetting the directors
And hard working committee,
We'll win the day and cry Hooray
For good old Raith F. C.

My Boy Tammy[37]

Whaur hae ye been aa the-day,
My boy Tammy?
Dae ye ken I'm waitin on yer pay,
My boy Tammy?
I've been doon in yon wee bar,
Wi drinking beer I'm aff the spar,
And I had a row amang the glaur,
My bonnie Mammy.

Did ye gaun to the fitba match,
My boy Tammy?
For on yer face ye wear a patch,
My ugly Tammy,
I've been seein the Rangers play,
And, by jings, they won the day,
The centre scored juist richt away,
My auld-fashioned Mammy.

Wha gied you the big black ee,
My boy Tammy?
Had ye a tussle wae the referee,
My hardy Tammy?
I got yin, but he got twaa,
The referee caaed Jock McCraw,
On a stretcher they carried him awaa,
Crying for his Mammy.

---

[37] This is a parody on the song which Robert Burns included in his collection for Johnson's *Scots Musical Museum* (1797–1893). The song, which he saw in a magazine in 1791, was attributed to Hector McNeil of Edinburgh, and Burns sent a revised version of 'My Boy Tammy' to Johnson, the editor, who had engaged classical composers for the project. Words and music are in Vol. VI, p. 518. The tune of this one is by Franz Joseph Haydn, and it has been recorded many times by classical singers.

When are ye gaun tae stop the drink,
My boy Tammy?
At nichts I canna sleep a wink,
My silly Tammy,
I think mysel I'll gie it up,
But no till oor team wins the cup,
Ye ken I want anither sup,
Tak pity on yer Tammy.

The Rale Mackay[38]

Tune: 'Wi a Hundred Pipers.'[39]

Ye've heard o oor piper, wee Bobby Mackay,
At Cowden sports he had a great try,
And he pleased the judges sae wonderfully fine,
As he played aa his tunes in the best o time.

CHORUS
Oh when he started tae blaw, tae blaw,
Wi his Stewart tartan kilt sae braw, sae braw,
From the Central Park he marched awaa,
Wi twaa first prizes, a third ane an aa.

Lang may he be able tae show his worth,
Play "The Barren Rocks" or "The Cock o the North",
And aye jine in wi the rest o the band,
When the pipe major gies the word o command.

---

[38] Footballer, sportsman and piper Robert 'Piper' Mackay was from Lochgelly. His father was Pipe-major of Hill of Beath Pipe Band and from 1926 to 1930 Robert was in the juvenile section of the band. A frequent prize winner at Highland games, he was also a competitive runner and keen footballer. He became a regimental piper with the Queen's Own Cameron Highlanders and served in West Africa, Italy and Greece. He became a sergeant in 1942 and in 1944, as Pipe Major of the 5th (Scottish) Battalion of the Parachute Regiment, parachuted into France with his bagpipes. After the war he was stationed in Inverness, where he won the Highland Society of London's Piobaireachd Gold Medal at Oban. In 1949, he re-joined his battalion in Tripoli and a year later was seconded to Khartoum where he instructed the pipers of the Sudan Defence Force. In 1952, he was Pipe Major in the Queen's Own Cameron Highlanders and again won the Highland Society of London's Gold Medal for Solo Piping that year in Inverness. As David Allen put it, Robert 'Piper' Mackay made a big noise in more than one field and his achievements really were something for Wee Bobby from Lochgelly to blaw about!

[39] Though no tune is suggested on the manuscript copy, MacLeod's words fit the rhythm of that well known song, and the chorus also echoes the text composed by Carolina Oliphant (Lady Nairne, 1766—1845).

And when they started tae blaw "Hooch aye!"
We'll carry wee Bobby shoulder high,
And gie three cheers for the "Rale Mackay",
And gae singing hame,"Hi Tiddly Hi".

The Trip Doon Tae Wembley O

Probably to the tune 'The Day We Went to Rothesay-O.'

I'm gaun tae say a word or twaa,
About me and my pal, Jock McCraw,
We dressed oorsels and went awaa,
Tae the International at Wembley,
O, It wis a grand trip, I am shair,
We made the Londoners aa stare,
We were fitbaa daft, I dae declare,
The day we gaed tae Wembley, O.

CHORUS
Fal-de-dal-the-doo-a-day,
Fal-the-dal-the-daddy-O,
Fal-the-dal-the do-a-day,
The day we gaed tae Wembley, O.

Wi tartan tammies on oor heid,
We landed in tae hae a feed,
They kent we were the Hielan breed,
When we gaed doon tae Wembley, O,
We had chappit tatties and London stew,
And Doch-an-doris, just a few,
Tae follow up the lads in blue,
We gaed awaa tae Wembley, O.

When oor team come on the field,
The roof and rafters aa did a reel,
Hoo the lads and lassies they did squeal,
Because they were at Wembley, O,
We thocht things were up the pole,
Till Tommy Walker scored a goal,
We aa went beyond control,
As we cheered oor boys at Wembley, O.

We would like tae gang back again,
For aa the fun comin in the train,
We joined in mony a sweet refrain,
On oor trip tae Wembley, O,
We wish oor Scots team aa the best,
They put the English tae the test,
Jerry Dawson and the rest,
They won the championship at Wembley, O.

Tribute Tae Willie Penman

The reliable goal-scorer of Raith Rovers F.C. Tune: 'A Wee Doch-an-Doris.'

We hae a dandy centre,
Willie Penman is his name,
And mony a bonnie goal he's scored
At this awfu fitbaa game.
He's very tricky on the baa,
And the croods frae far and near
When they see him trip oot on the field
'Tis then they start tae cheer.

CHORUS
  Come away, Willie Penman,
  Ye're playing the game sae fine,
  And leading the van aa ye can,
  The Rovers' wee front line.
  You've scored goals tae yer credit,
  And may ye keep it up,
  And help the lads in navy blue tae win the League Cup.

Tae see him dodgin wi the baa
I'm shair its juist a treat;
The half-back and the back, ye ken,
He leaves them in Queer Street,
And when he gets a chance at goal
He's as busy as can be;
So guid luck tae Willie Penman
O the good old Raith F.C.

Tribute Tae Willie Waddell

or the 'Glesga' Rangers F.C.' Tune: 'Heilan Laddie.'

Wha can play the game sae braw?
Willie Waddell, Willie Waddell,
Wha's a demon on the baa?
Slippy Willie Waddell.
When he's flying doon the wing,
And gets the baa on the swing,
Mony a braw goal it daes bring,
Tricky Willie Waddell.

Wha can lead the backs a dance?
Willie Waddell, Willie Waddell,
As down the field he daes prance,
Pushing Willie Waddell.
He put ower a bonnie square,
Just tae find Willie Thornton there,
Anither goal I do declare,
Frae dandy Willie Waddell.

Wha is he the croods adore?
Willie Waddell, Willie Waddell,
As through the defence he daes bore,
Speedy Willie Waddell.
He's been a Rangers staunch and true
Wears the jersey o light blue,
Wha deserves a medal noo?,
Oor ain Willie Waddell.

We're Oot Tae Win The Day

Tune: 'A Wee Drapie Mair.'

The cup-tie craze comes yince a year,
'Tis then we try oor best,
We follow up oor favourite team
We think far abune the rest.
Wi oor crawmills and oor colours
We mak the grandstand ring,
And when they score we start tae roar,
And this is what we start tae sing:

CHORUS
    Hurry up and play the baa,
    Bang it frae wing tae wing,
    Pass it tae the centre noo
    And see what it will bring,
    Let him drive it for the goal,
    Ye'll find that's his best play;
    Watch yer game and the cup ye'll claim,
    For we're oot tae win the day.

Oor goalie he's a champion,
He's no sae easily beat,
Oor backs they are a sturdy pair,
Their kickin is just a treat,
The half-back line is up tae time,
They ken maist every prank,
They work like electricity,
Oor dashing wee front rank.

And if we chance tae win the cup,
It will be a grand affair,
We'll tak oor hats juist like that
And toss them in the air,
We'll gie the players a herty shake,
The cup we'll cairry shoulder high,
We'll aa gang merry hame at nicht,
And no forget tae cry:

CHORUS

Oor Champion George McCrae

Tune: 'Give my love to Nancy.'

Oh have ye seen oor little peds?
They caa him George McCrae,
At running a long distance
He's the marvel o the day,
In his braw strip he looks a tip,
As on the track he speeds his way;
The crowds they admire him,
And this is what they say:

CHORUS

Noo come away, wee George McCrae,
We like tae see yer style;
Wi a graceful stride ye're Scotland's pride,
Ye can fairly go yer mile,
We hiv guid runners on the turf,
But they aa fade away
Frae this wee block o auld Bank-knock,
Oor champion George McCrae.

At auld Motherwell ye went pell-mell
Yer rinnin was juist a treat;
Ye beat yer men there and then,
Man, it was a splendid feat!
Lang may ye prance and toe the line,
As the tape ye mak it sway,
And be ready for Jean Vermeulen,
Oor wee champion George McCrae.

CHORUS

The Empire Skating Rink

I'm a chap that's fond of skating,
So just listen yin and aa
I took a trip tae the Empire Rink,
Tae see the sichts sae braw,
The moment I got in the place,
My hert was filled with glee,
I wis juist aboot tae tak a seat,
When a girl cried oot tae me.

CHORUS
   We're Skating, Skating,
   Skating all the time,
   We're Rinking, Rinking,
   Oh what a pantomime
   When the boys go rolling on the floor,
   They give their girls the wink,
   And seem tae say, "O come away!"
   At the Empire Skating Rink.

Juist then I donned a pair o skates,
But I thocht them awfu queer,
I got on the track, they aa stood back,
For I was fleeing like a deer
But aa at yince I made a smash,
When trying some fancy reels,
The Manager picked me aff the flair,
And said "Mind that ye're on wheels."

CHORUS

At the Fancy Dress Carnival,
The folk at me did stare,
I wis dressed up as the 'Real MacKay',
Wi my Shepherd Tartan hair,
I shook hands wi the bold Rob Roy
And likewise Kate the Tink,
There's fun galore on the floor,
At the Empire Skating Rink.

CHORUS

The Whuppet Race

Did ye ever visit the North End Park,
Tae see the duggies rin
Baith big and smaa among them aa,
They dae their best tae win.
As shair as Setterday nicht comes roond,
They ken withoot a doubt,
The moment that they toe the mark,
It's then ye hear them shout:

CHORUS
    Ha-wey-lass, ha-wey-lass,
    Ye're shair tae hear them cry,
    Ha-wey-lad, ha-wey-lad,
    Come on and hae a try!
    For if ye win this handicap,
    I'm gaun tae change yer name,
    And ye'll get a pund o steak the nicht,
    When ye gang hame.

There's the Drummer and the Piper,
Lady Lake and Gipsy Tam,
There's J.J. frae Lochgelly tae,
And likewise Peter Pan,
There's Black Rose and there's Kelly,
Stop the Cab for wee Black Nell,
And when the pistol gaes off,
The owners they do yell.

CHORUS

Tae see them fleeing up the field,
Man, it's a bonnie sicht,
And when they mooth the hankie,
They think themselves aa richt,
Wi their leaders and their muzzles,
And wee flannel overall,
It causes great excitement,
When the bookies start tae bawl:

CHORUS

And when the race is ower again,
They wander doon the street,
And offer tae stand their hand,
Tae ony yin they meet,
For my dug won the handicap,
So I'll treat ye if ye're game,
I'll train him up for Setterday next,
And ye'll hear me shout again.

CHORUS

War

Dark Neuve Chapelle[40]

Tune: 'Dark Lochnagar.'

Come aa ye gallant heroes wha fought wi the tartan,
Juist a word o praise for the laddies that are gone;
Nae wonder the saut tear in oor ee gangs a-sparklin,
When we think on those faces we ne'er shall look upon.
They fought and died for their country sae dearly,
And those that returned mony's a sad story tell;
They left their dear homes and aa they loved sincerely,
Noo they sleep in a cauld grave roun Dark Neuve Chapelle.

These brave sons o Scotland wherever they gaither,
We'll honour their names, their duty they've done.
They were reared in the land o the bonnie purple heather,
And faced the bloody foe men in victories won.
But a fond mother's love is tenderly keeping,
Her hert fu o grief for it's breakin in twa[41]
When she thinks on her braw lad, wha calmly lies sleeping,
Side by side wi his comrades roun Dark Neuve Chapelle.

---

[40] The Battle of Neuve Chapelle was 10–13 March, 1915, during which there were more than 11,000 casualties.

[41] Line missing from manuscript copy, so this is a suggested replacement.

The Tartan My Daddy Wore at Mons[42]

A little boy and girl coming home from school
Where they had been taught the golden rule,
The boy to the little maid did say,
"Guess what the scholars were asking me to-day?"
"Why does little Mary wear that old fashioned shawl?
Daily she's admired by one and all."
But Mary only shook her little head –
With tears in her eyes to the boy she said:

CHORUS
　　"That's the tartan my daddy wore at Mons,
　　Facing a mighty foe;
　　When they cried for men he volunteered then
　　Yes, he was among the first to go.
　　He fell like a Briton, brave and true,
　　Fighting for dear home and little ones;
　　I'll tell the scholars all, I love this old plaid shawl,
　　That's the tartan my daddy wore at Mons."

He kissed me good-bye before he went away
And said he'd come back to me and mother some day
But sad was the news when the letter it came:
We learned that daddy had numbered with the slain
And his old tartan kilt was sent to me
From France far over the sea;
With a lock of his hair, I'll treasure with care,
And for my daddy's sake this shawl I'll wear.

---

[42] The Battle of Mons was 23 August 1914, and was the first battle of the Great War, which had been declared on August 4.

Scotland

The Auld Scotch Sangs[43]

O Sing tae me the Auld Scotch Sangs
And I'll Row thee Ower the Clyde,
The Day we Went tae Rothesay-O
Doon by the River Side.
Wha sang Wha'll Buy ma Herrin?
The Stoutest Man in Forty-twaa,
Where Are the Boys o the Old Brigade,
Noo they're far, far awaa.

There's Nae Luck About the Hoose,
And so We'd Bide a Wee,
For Annie Laurie ran awaa
Wi the Piper o Dundee.
Will Ye no Come Back Again?
Said Dainty Davie wi a smile.
O Whistle and I'll Come Tae ye My Lad,
Said the Lass o Ballochmyle.

Sing on, sing mair, O Scotland Yet,
Bring tae Me a Pint o Wine.
My Hert is Sair for Somebody
In the Auld Hoose – Hame o Mine.
There was a Lad was Born in Kyle,
Where Scotland Found her Fame
Should Auld Acquaintance be Forgot,
O Why Left I my Hame?

---

[43] 'O sing to Me the Old Scotch Songs' was composed in the late 1800's by Rev. George W. Bethune and Joseph Frederick Leeson, and published in collections such as The Morwen Collection of Scottish Songs, With Accompaniments for Piano (Mozart Allan, 1895). It became a fireside favourite the world over, particularly after Harry Lauder recorded it in 1925 on RCA Victor's 78 rpm record (45256), as side B, with 'Bonnie Mary of Argyle' on side A. The copy among MacLeod's papers was written out in 4-line verses, but as that would not fit the melody, the verses here are printed as 8-line stanzas, which, if sung to the original tune, would require repetition of lines 7 and 8. In the twenty-first century, MacLeod's composition would be a gift to folk who organize pub 'Quiz Nights'.

The Banks o Clyde[44]

On the banks o the Clyde
Stood a lad and his lassie;
The lad's name wis Geordie
Ye maist understand.
He was bound for a foreign land.
Up aboot Kirkcaldy,
Wi a sword in his teeth
And a brick in each hand.

CHORUS
Over the burning plains o Dysart,
Fighting away like fools,
Scrapping under Union Jack,
Or the Miners Federation rules;
Chasing the deid home tae their bed,
Nobody felt the least afraid,
And that's how a lamplighter got his position.
He was one of the light brigade.

---

[44] If MacLeod sang the song 'to the tune of...' there is a sense that he may have used two – one for the verses and another for the chorus, which does not have the same meter as the verses. Though no tune is suggested, , the opening line and title echo the poignant song of the same opening line, 'The Blantyre Explosion' 1877. Though that song is about a terrible tragedy, it is not unusual for a song-maker or entertainer to detract from the agonies of life by trying to make folk smile again. Several studies deal with such issues: See, Mary Beth Stein, 'The Politics of Humour: The Berlin Wall in Jokes and Graffiti' in Western Folklore, vol. XLVIII, pp. 85-108; Robert Cochran, "WHAT COURAGE!' Romanian 'Our Leader' Jokes', Journal of American Folklore, Vol. 102, No. 405, pp. 259-274; Willie Smyth, 'Challenger Jokes and the Humour of Disaster' in Western Folklore Vol. XLV, No. 4, 243-260; Elizabeth Radin Simons, 'The NASA Joke Cycle: The Astronauts and the Teacher' in Western Folklore Vol. XLV, No. 4 , pp. 261-277.

Though a gas tank divided
The lad from his lassie,
Though Geordie was forced
Tae drink beer without foam,
His thochts o scotch haggis,
Stovies, tatties, and herring,
And the row he'd get frae Jean
He left greetin at hame.

When Geordie came hame
The hoose was deserted,
Naethin but pawn tickets
Scattered ower the flair,
And a line on the bunker,
Read "Died broken herted",
But she had fled wi another,
Jean juist dyed her hair.

The Big Camlachie Slope[45]

My name is Geordie McIntosh,
I'm a member o the Force,
I come frae auld Camlachie,
Whaur I yist tae drive a horse,
But noo I got another job,
I'm oot there driving men,
And I like tae see the street aa clear
At 10 p.m.

CHORUS
As I walk doon the street wi my pancake feet
The bairns ken, I'm always on the hop,
They aa cry after me, "Ye couldnae catch a flea,
Ten-taed McIntosh, the big Camlachie slope."

I never try tae lift a man
That's as big as me,
I happened for tae try it yince,
It proved ower much for me,
We wrestled for twaa hours an mair,
I found I had nae show,
I kindly asked who had trained him,
"O," said he, "it wis Munro."

CHORUS

---

[45] Though no tune is suggested, the song is reminiscent of 'The Buchan Bobbie' composed by George S. Morris (1876–1980), who recorded for Beltona Records.

I'm in love wi aa the ladies[46]
For miles aroun the place,
It's worth their while tae get a smile
O my sonsie Hielan face.
But there's yin I like abin the rest
Caaed Mary Ann McGee,
Tae tell the truth she's crazy
On the big P.C.

---

[46] The manuscript copy had 'slaveys'.

The Bonnie Banks o Loch Lomond Parody[47]

By yon bonnie banks whaur I lost aa ma claes,
Whaur the waters are lukewarm in Loch Lomond,
I went in for a dook, and my claes took their hook
Frae the bonnie, bonnie banks o Loch Lomond.

CHORUS
 I couldnae tak the high road, I daurnae tak the low road,
 Wi anger at the mooth I wis foamin',
 I wis shivering frae the cauld till my heid it turned bald,
 On the bonnie, bonnie banks o Loch Lomond.

I sat doon aa my lane and I thocht hoo I'd get hame
When I saw a figure comin thro the gloamin;
A lassie came in sicht, so I ran wi aa my micht
Roon aboot the bonnie banks o Loch Lomond.

She cried, "Oh dearie Mac, Oh hurry and come back,
And roon the cunnin stane we'll gang a-roamin,
For Adam he met Eve, wi nae claes, I believe,
On the bonnie, bonnie banks o Loch Lomond."

---

[47] There are several parodies of 'Loch Lomond' including a different one that was popularised by by music-hall comedian Jock McKendrick, who recorded it (c. 1934) on Perthshire label, Great Scott Records.

The Glesga Folks For Fun

Tune: Original.

There is a time o year comes roon,
Wi me ye will agree,
When Glesca folk fairly flock,
Doon by the briny sea.
They leave auld Glesca on the Clyde,
Tae spend their holiday,
When they meet wi ane anither,
Oh! this is what they say.

CHORUS

"Dae ye come frae the Cowcaddens,
Or guid auld Sauchiehall?
Are ye oot here on yer own,
Tae act the lah-de-dah?"
Wi dancin and singin there,
By jings they tak the bun,
I see nae folk like Glesca folk,
They are the folk for fun.

There's Jock and Jean and Tam and Nan,
They are prancin doon the street,
And offering tae stand their hand,
Tae cronies that they meet.
"Come on Jock, gie's a slider,
Or some tatties in a poke,"
Tae treat his lass aff eighteen bob,
Whit dae ye think o Jock?

The Laddies Wha Followed the Ploo[48]

My name is Johnnie Tamson, a plooman I'm made,
For thirty lang years I hae followed my trade,
I attended my duties, an there's quite a few,
And we're aa jolly laddies wha follow the ploo.

CHORUS
  Tra-la-la, tra-la-lee and hoo wad ye,
  Hoo wad ye, hoo wad ye like tae be me?

I rise in the morning at quarter tae five,
Tae mak sure aa my beasties are healthy and thrive,
Frae my wee pet yowie tae my favorite black coo,
For we're aa jolly laddies wha follow the ploo.

On ilk market day I dress mysel braw,
The lassies they adore me baith big and smaa,
We gang through a Scotch Reel and the 'Bunnets o Blue'
For we're aa jolly laddies wha follow the ploo.

I gaed intae a wee pub tae hae a bit drink,
When a saucy wee lassie at me she did wink,
She said, "Ye're a nice chappie," as nearer she drew,
But she couldnae catch Johnnie wha follows the ploo.

---

[48] Though no tune is suggested, it fits the well-known tune of 'Villikins and his Dinah' (Laws M31A/B and Roud 271), popular in MacLeod's day. As this is also the tune used for 'The Ould Orange Flute', MacLeod may also have known that song. In Scotland, singers today may be more familiar with recent songs to the same tune such as 'The Wee Magic Stane' and 'The Turra Coo'.

Say I, "Noo wee lassie, I've a wife o my ain,
Three bonnie bairnies ad a cosy wee hame,
I'm thinking on Jeannie, she'll be milking the noo,
And singing aboot her laddie wha follows the ploo."

Awaa wi yer grandeur and aa thing like that,
Yer swallow-tail coat, yer chocker and hat,
He's the pride o the land wi his coat o dark blue,
And they're aa jolly laddies who follow the ploo.

Scots Wha Hae

With Apologies.[49]

Scots wha hae on oatcakes fed,
Ye've lost the road yer faithers led,
When Scotland brawny clansmen bred,
But not on buns and tea.

Yer Scottish grit has flown awa
Ye've scarce a soond tooth in yer jaw
If Scotland's glory ye'd recaa
Tak Oatcakes noo wi me.

Wha wid be a silly knave
As aye tae pastries be a slave?
He's sure tae fill an early grave.
Let him droop an dee.

If you'd regain auld Scotland's power,
Don't hesitate anither hour,
Discard the trashy sugared flour
An tak Oatcakes wi me.

Nae wonder ye hae aches an pains,
Wi scanty flesh on shrunken banes.
If ye wid rear braw sturdy weans,
Be advised by me.

Ye'll strike disease a fatal blow,
Yer bairnie's cheecks wi health will glow,
An win first prize in ony show,
Try Capital Oatcakes an see!

---

[49] The Broadsheet was printed by Thomas Adams & Sons, Printers, Portobello. Below the poem is the inscription: "Printed to acknowledge our gratitude to the admirer of our Capital Oatcakes who sent in this parody."

"Scots Wha Hae"

(With Apologies).

Scots wha ance on oatcakes fed,
Ye've lost the road ye'r faithers led,
When Scotland brawny clansmen bred,
But not on buns and tea.

Ye'r Scottish grit hae flown awa',
Ye've scarce a soond tooth in ye'r jaw,
If Scotland's glory ye'd reca'
Tak' Oatcakes noo wi' me.

Wha wid be a silly knave,
As aye tae pastries be a slave,
He's sure tae fill an early grave,
Let him droop an' dee.

If you'd regain auld Scotland's power,
Don't hesitate anither hour,
Discard the trashy sugared flour,
An' tak' Oatcakes wi' me.

Na wonder ye ha'e aches an' pains,
Wi' scanty flesh on shrunken banes,
If ye wid rear braw sturdy weans,
Be advised by me;

Ye'll strike disease a fatal blow,
Ye'r bairnie's cheeks wi' health will glow,
An' win first prize at ony show,
Try " Capital Oatcakes " and see.

Printed to acknowledge our gratitude to the unknown admirer of our Capital
Oatcakes who sent in this parody.

Thomas Adams & Sons, Printers, Portobello.

The Scotch Merry Widda

I'm a handsome merry widda,
From London all the way,
I took a trip tae my native land,
For tae spend a holiday,
I've brocht the latest styles in hats,
For tae let the ladies see,
But the lads in Bonnie Scotland
Fairly tak a len o me.

CHORUS
They tak my hat, on it they sat,
They tore oot aa my hair,
But when I gae back tae London,
I can trim up plenty mair,
Though I was born in Scotland,
And brought up in Ballochmyle,
I am gaun tae London yince a year,
Tae bring oot the latest style.

Noo when I landed in this place,
The croods aroon me flocked,
And when they saw my braw new hat
They laughed, they sang, they joked,
The bairns they aa run after me,
My heart went pit-a-pat,
They were overjoyed, when they destroyed
My new Merry Widda Hat.

CHORUS

I then stopped all the traffic,
As I walked along the street,
I even stopped two Bobbies,
That were busy on the beat,

But then they apprehended me,
For causing such a din,
They locked the Merry Widda up,
Weel I think it was a sin.

CHORUS

When I get back tae London gay,
I'll tell the Scotch folk there,
The style o ma hat they didnae like,
It's the Tammy that they wear,
Tae the Scotch knit is becoming,
For it fairly taks the cake,
If I come back wi such a hat
I'll mak a big mistake.

CHORUS

Sketches, Monologues, Patter, and the Last Word

DEPEND ON YER DOCTOR
A Scots Comedy Sketch
BY
Robert MacLeod

(CHARACTERS)

Meg McPherson --------------------A Sair Tried Woman
Jock McPherson -------------------- A Thochtless Man
Lizzie McPherson ------------------Their Dochter
Dr. McNab ------------------------- A Kind Hearted Physician

ACT (1)

Scene: Kitchen of the McPhersons House – Bed, Table, Dresser and Two Chairs

"Meg" McPherson (Lying in Bed). Aweel, aweel, I needna say I'm weel either, for I'm neither like weel nor woe, and nae wonder, for its trouble, trouble, trouble in this hoose frae mornin' till nicht, and aa ower the heid o this man o mine, Jock McPherson, the ne'er-dae-weel. He'll neither work nor want as the saying goes. Jock McPherson yist tae be a hard workin, pushin man, but I ken what he'll be pushin afore lang. It'll be a candy barrie. Aye, but I'll mak him work, supposin I should get a bottle for him, but it'll no be the spirit o Henry Tamson, mind I'm tellin ye.

Lizzie McPherson: (Enters, tidying up the house).Weel, mither hoo are ye this mornin. Did ye sleep weel last nicht, and did yon daisy poother dae ye ony guid I gied ye before I gaed the bed?

Meg: Daisy poother Lizzie! Haud yer tongue lassie. I think I'll sune be in below the daisies aa the gather. Weel my heid's a wee bit better, but there's an awfu heaviness at my breist, jist the same as somebody wis knockin at my kist wi a hammer.

Lizzie: Oh, mither, its worry that's wrang wi ye, and if ye wid only content yersel mair. I think it wid be better for ye.

Meg: Content mysel, Lizzie! Hoo can I content mysel, lassie, and yer faither gaun aboot idle and the rent rinnin on, and aa thing else? Michty me! I'll sune be awa tae a sheddie: I think I'll sune be aff my heid aa thegither.

Lizzie: But mither, ye'll ha tae gie my faither time tae look for a job, for ye ken jobs are no sae easy tae get the noo, mind ye that.

Meg: Aye lassie, I ken the time he'll be daein afore lang, he'll be daein time ower in Saughton for keepin a no-weel wumman lyin here withoot supportin her. But Lizzie, folk say prevention is better than cure so when ye get the hoose redd-up, jist gang awa doon and leave word for Dr. McNab tae come up tae yer mither. He's an awfu fine man, and aye been very attentive tae me in time o trouble. So jist dae that. Hurry noo, Lizzy, lassie.

Lizzie: And what will I pit on mither?

Meg: Och, Lizzie, jist pit on yer mither's auld tartan shawl.

Lizzie: And if I see my faither, what will I say if he asks
me whaur I'm gaun?

Meg: Och ay, he's awa doon for his dole money, I
daresay, ay awa doon for his dole money. Weel,
Lizzie, jist tell him ye're awa doon for thruppence-
worth o pork ribs tae mak some beef-tea for yer
mither. Ye see Lizzie, I dinna want him tae ken
that I'm sendin for the doctor ava. I jist want tae
fricht him Lizzie, so hurry you awaa, lassie.

Lizzie: Aa richt mither, I'll no be lang.

(Lizzie hurries for the doctor)

Meg: Guidness me, the men noo-a-days wid bring years
on an auld buddy. But I'll ask Dr. McNab when
he comes tae veesit me tae gie me a line aff his
hand tae the effect that Jock McPherson has tae
get a job, reason or nane, as he has a no-weel wife
tae support. It micht dae aa the guid in the world,
and ye hiv tae dae something tae fricht them, oh,
aye. But, wheest, wheest, here comes wanderin
Steenie.

(Jock McPherson enters, half-drunk and singing)

Ay, are ye sleepin' Maggie?
Oh! Are ye sleepin' Maggie?
Open the door for lood the win'
Is blawin' ower the Warlock Craggie.

Meg: Aye, I ken whit door will be open for you afore
lang, it'll be the jile door, and the wind'll no blaw
on ye there, ye lazy scroondrel. Hiv ye haen a
board the day or what, or hae ye got a job yet?

Jock: Naw, naw Maggie, I hivna faa'en in yet, wumman.

Meg: No, ye hivna faa'en in yet, but if I hiv my guide
              ee sicht, I think ye've faa'en intae some place yer
              very seldom oot o, you and yer bloomin cronies.
              Ye think far mair o' them than yer wife and hame,
              ye ne'er-dae-weel, ye! I mind ye said ye widna
              gie me for the warld, but noo I'm thinkin ye wid
              gie me awa for a bawbie balloon. Aye, Jock, if I'd
              been fed as weel's I've been stairved, I'd been a
              braw wumman. But wait till I get up oot o this
              bed, I'll gie you a proper doin, or my name's no
              Meg McPherson. Whaur's yer dole money, eh!
              Aye, dish it oot. Whit ye hiv onywey, I ken it's no
              muckle.

Jock: (Handing Meg his dole money) There ye are
              Maggie, and content yersel wumman. I'll get a job
              bye-and-bye.

Meg: Ay, ay, it'll jist be Bye-and Bye.

(Sings Sweet Bye-and-Bye)

              Imphm, seventeen shillings. That's yours, but
              whaurs mine and Lizzie's. Whit hiv I tae dae wi
              this noo? It widna buy Lark Mixture for a Canary,
              Jock. Ye've shairly been weetin yer whussel the
              day I'm thinkin eh! Whaur's the rent?

Jock: Weel Maggie, ye ken we'll hae tae pey the tiler for
              my claes, and ha'en the wee drap in me wummin, I
              couldna pass the man's door withoot gaun in and
              gien him something. I'm honest enough, mind ye,
              Maggie, supposin I hivna a job tae gang tae.

Meg: I ken fine ye hivna a job tae gang tae; that's the
                wey yer gaun aboot idle. Jock, ye've neither thocht
                nor care aboot yer puir wife ava.

(Enter Lizzie. Back from the docter's)

Lizzie: Oh, aye, there ye are the twa o ye, fightin, as usual.
                Mercy me! There's mair rows than scones in this
                hoose!

Meg: Ay, Lizzie, and ye'll no get muckle scones either, if
                this man gangs on the wey he's daein. Dae ye ken
                whit he's dune.

Lizzie: No me mither.

Meg: He's caa'd intae Broon the tiler and gien him five
                shillings aff his dole money, and me lyin here like
                a paper angel for the want o support. But he didna
                forget tae steep his ain lips wi his boozin cronies
                before he came intae the hoose.

Lizzie: (Looking astonished) Ye shairly didna dae that
                faither, and my mither lyin here no weel. Ach,
                man ye should let him wait till ye got a job; the
                tiler's no deein for his money, supposin he dyes
                claes.

Jock: Aweel Lizzie, I thocht it the best plan lassie, ye'll
                hae heard o the auld sayin, Lizzie: "Oot o debt, oot
                o danger."

Meg: Ay, that's richt enough Jock, but ye'll no be oot o
                danger if I'm spared tae get up oot this bed. Mind
                I'm tellin ye. Aweel, Jock McPherson, ye can jist
                gang awa doon tae Broon the tiler, and get back

that five shillings ye gied him. We're faur mair in need o it than the tiler at this present time, and foreby, there's somebody comin tae veesit me the day, and I wad like quietness for a wee while, so awa ye go; and if ye get the five shillings, see and bring it hame tae the hoose, and no gang awa again wi yer boozin cronies and swallow it, or mind ye there'll be some fun in this hoose when ye dae come back.

Lizzie: Aye, faither, gang awa and dae whit my mither wants ye tae dae. I'll hae tae get the hoose cleaned up for the veesitor comin. And mind and no let the public-hoose sign fa doon on the tap o ye.

Jock: Oh, aye, ye're gettin a veesitor are ye Lizzie. Is it the doctor or wha?

Meg: Never you mind Jock, ye'll maybe ken aa aboot it when ye come back, if ye dinna get that five shillings frae the tiler.

Jock: Weel, I'll awa doon and try him, and if I dae get it, and meet ony o my cronies, they'll be bitin my lug for me tae stand my hand, for ye ken Meg, 'When freens meet, Hearts warm.'

Meg: Aye, and there'll be a warm reception waitin on you when ye come back, if ye dae sic a thing. Awaa ye go noo, and look for a job when ye're oot. Awaa ye go and na haud the nerves takin the better o' me.

Jock: Oh, I'm gaun; gie me time.

(Lighting his pipe)

Meg: Aye, ye'll get time richt enough.

Lizzie   Rushes at Jock saying: Gang awa faither and no haud my mither fleein' intae they raptures, or she micht tak ane o' they sick turns ye ken.

(Meg takes a sick turn and faints back on bed, crying: "Lizzie Lizzie".)

Lizzie rushes at her father saying: Aye, ye've dune it noo, haven't ye?

Jock: Awa lassie, yer mither hisna faintit, his she?

Lizzie: (running over to the bed and looking at her mother) Aye, faither, she's clean awaa; my mither's faintit clean awaa.

(Jock stands astonished looking over at bed.)

Curtain.

End of Act 1

ACT 2

Meg: (Sitting in chair waiting for the doctor.) Noo I'm feelin a bit sickish after that turn I taen; aye, dear, I wish that doctor wid come. Haw, Lizzie!

Lizzie: (Coming running in) Oh mither! As I lookit oot the scullery winda, I see the doctor's car staunin doon the raw a bit. He'll be intae some hoose doon there, and he'll be here directly.

Meg: Hurry then, Lizzie; get aa the things tidied up, for ye ken Dr. McNab likes tae see aa thing fine and clean lassie.

Lizzie: (Hearing rap at the door)

That's him at the door mither.

Meg: Go on then, Lizzie, and be mannerable and say, "Good-after-noon, Doctor," when ye open the door.

(Doctor Enters with bag in hand)

Doctor: Good afternoon. Goodness gracious Mrs McPherson! It's you that's the patient, is it?

Meg: Aye, doctor, it's me. The wey I sent for ye wis really tae see whit's wrang wi me.

Dr.:   (Laying down his hat and bag.) Well, Mrs McPherson, I'll have a proper examination of you. How are you feeling at all? Let me see your tongue, please.

(Meg puts out her tongue.)

Dr.:   Imphm! It's a little coated I see.

Meg: A little coated! Weel it shouldna be doctor, for I hivna eaten a bite these three days.

Dr.:   But, Mrs McPherson, people as a rule don't eat much when they're in trouble you know.

Meg: No, I believe that doctor; but ye canna get it tae eat in this hoose when yer weel, never mind when yer in trouble. Oh Dear! I've an awfu sair kist, Doctor.

Dr.:   Well, Mrs. McPherson, we'll soon hear what's wrong with your chest. I always carry instruments with me, you know, so I'll have you sounded.

Meg: Oh dear! The last time ye sounded me doctor, wis when the flu flew over frae France.

Meg: (Continuing) Dae ye mind o' that doctor? I doot it's a blue doo wi' me this time.

Dr.:   (Sounding Mrs McPherson) Oh, yes there's a wee wheetsle at your chest.

Meg: (Getting annoyed) A wee wheasle! Oh Lizzie, Lizzie, bring in the dug: there's a wee wheasle at yer mither's breist.

Dr.:   Oh, no! I don't mean that! I mean a little huskiness, or heaviness, at your chest.

Meg: I'm gled o that, Doctor; I thocht I wis sent for the noo.

Dr: Once again, Mrs McPherson; just to hear what's

going on inside.

Meg: There's shairly naething wrang inside, Doctor. I'm
          gettin nervous when ye say that.

Dr.:   Well, I've come to the conclusion, Mrs McPherson,
          that it's a nervous breakdown.

Meg: Ay, dear me, I jist thocht it. I'll sune be broken up
          in bits, and it's aa ower the heid o this man o mine
          no workin and gaun aboot drinkin.

Dr.:   Is John McPherson not working?

Meg: No him. Wark's no in his heid. He's like the
          man that went tae look for wark, he's prayin tae
          guideness he'll no find it.

Dr.:   And he drinks, you say?

Meg: Drinks! Aye, like a fish, doctor; he wad drink the
          sea dry and turn ower the rocks for mair, and he's
          no carin whether I sink or sweem.

Dr.:   Well, Mrs McPherson, I'm going to give you the
          best bottle I can, and I'm sure it will get you all
          right in a day or so and you'll be as well as ever
          again.

Meg: Oh thank ye doctor. Oh, thank ye.

(Doctor makes out line for medicine)

Dr.:   It's the old cough mixture, with two drachms of –

Meg: Haud there doctor, I hope its no drams o whiskey,

for if Jock McPherson comes in, I'll no hae a ghost
o a chance o it; he'll lick it clean oot after me, as
shair as daith, Doctor.

Dr.:   Oh, no, Mrs McPherson, its just two drachms of
sarsaparilla to warm you up: and don't forget to
take a good big table-spoonful when you feel the
huskiness coming on.

Dr. to Lizzie: Now Miss McPherson, you know the chemist I
get my drugs from, just round the corner of the
street yonder.

Lizzie: Yes, Doctor.

Dr.:   Tell him to give it to you as soon as possible, and
hurry back with it.

(Lizzie hurries off)

Meg: I dinna ken whit I'd dae withoot that lassie, Doctor.
Ye ken whit I wis gaun tae ask ye for, Doctor?

Dr.:   I can't guess, Mrs. McPherson

Meg: Weel, I wis wantin a line aff yer haund for Jock tae
tak doon tae the Labour Exchange, tae see if he can
get a job ony quicker, as he his a no-weel wife tae
support.

Dr.:   Well, I'll do that, but I'll not say it will get him a job
any quicker, though it might help him in a way.

(Doctor makes out line.)

Meg: Ye'll hae quite a lot o patients the noo doctor, and ye'll hae tae hae an awfu patience wi them, I think, eh, Doctor.

Dr.:   Oh, yes, quite a lot Mrs McPherson. Now there you are; that line might do John a lot of good.

Meg: Oh, thank ye doctor, and I hope it will, for he's a hopeless case, is Jock. (Puts line below her shawl)

Dr.:   Well now, I must be going, and don't forget what I've told you.

(Doctor meets Lizzie coming in) Ah! You've got it all right.

Lizzie: Yes doctor. (Showing him bottle)

Dr.:   That's the stuff for her, and keep her quiet whatever you do. Well, good-bye, Mrs McPherson.

Meg: Guid-bye. Ta-ta, Doctor.

(Doctor goes away)

TWO PAGES MISSING[1]

resumes at point where Jock has returned home.

Lizzie: That's my mither's bottle; ye'll hae got yours afore the noo, I suppose. (Puts bottle back on dresser) Ye've shairly turned an awfu drouth, Faither.

---

[1] Despite the missing pages, it seems worth including the piece, if only to give the sense of the style of village-hall sketch that was popular in MacLeod's day. If anyone has a copy of the original, we would be very pleased to include it in any future edition.

| Meg: | Aye, Lizzie, when he'll drink my very medicine. Draw him ower tae this chair Lizzie, and I'll tell him something that's no guid for him; I find that whussle comin on again Lizzie, so jist gie me anither drap o my bottle, lassie, tae see if it'll rise the steam. |

(Lizzie give her mother medicine)

| Meg: | Heh! That's strong lassie. |

| Jock: | It's shairly guid stuff, Meg. |

| Meg: | Ay, Jock, it's fechtin stuff, so watch yersel! Whaur's the five shillings ye went tae get frae the tiler? |

| Jock: | Weel, Meg, I got the money richt enough, but jist as I wis comin oot o the man's door, the cronies wis waitin on me, and enticed me intae the pub tae hae a game at the dominoes; so in we went. |

| Meg: | And noo it's spent. |

| Jock: | Jist that, Meg; it's awaa like the rest. |

| Meg: | And did ye look for wark when ye wis oot? |

| Jock: | No me, Meg; there's plenty workin for naething withoot me startin tae work, wumman. |

| Meg: | (Producing a line from under her shawl) Weel Jock, here's a line a got frae Dr. McNab, tae the effect ye hiv tae get a job. Tak it, and awa doon tae the Labour Exchange wi it. Here, tak it. |

| Jock: | Its nae use tae me Meg. |

Meg: Weel, I jist feel the noo I could rise and gie ye a sair hidin. Aye, and ye'll get it tae. Gie me a wee drap mair oot that bottle Lizzie, it's the only stuff that's helpin me.

Lizzie: Here ye are mither, its fairly gaun doon.

Meg: Hic! That's the pale tartan.

There wis some news o me gaun tae the Infirmary, Jock, but its no me that's gaun, it's you; so we'll jist hae tae end it or mend it.

(Meg gets off chair in confusion, and grips Jock by the neck)

(Knock heard at the door)

Lizzie: Oh, mither, there's somebody at the door!

(Lizzie runs to answer the door)

Meg: See wha it is then Lizzie; maybe it's the doctor and me like this.

Lizzie: No, mither, its no the doctor.

Meg: Weel, is it the polis, Lizzie?

Lizzie: No Mither.

Meg: (Excited) An wha is it, Lizzie?

Lizzie: Twa men tae see if ye can gie them onything for the Infirmary.

Meg: Aye, Lizzie, tell them we'll gie them yer faither efter I'm dune wi him.

(Meg and Lizzie draw Jock along the stage and give him a doing.)

(CURTAIN)

THE END

A SCOTS DRAMA IN ONE ACT
"LOVE ON THE FARM"

The pages that follow show a facsimile version of this play. In MacLeod's day, village-hall sketches performed by amateur dramatic clubs were a very popular form of entertainment all over Scotland. Regional dialects were well represented, particularly in the North-East, after the appearance of Gavin Greig's well-known piece, *The Main's Wooin': A Drama of Northern Rural Life*. Written in the late 1800's, it became so popular that it was published (Peterhead, 1909 and Aberdeen: D. Wylie, 1912). Several sketches were written for women players as they were much in demand by the SWRI, which held fund-raisers and competitions, with songs and home-baking as part of the attraction. MacLeod includes both, and as the dialect in this sketch is reminiscent of the North-East production, it seems worth including a short example from Gavin Greig:

JOHN ANDERSON: (laying down newspaper) Ye're unco quaet the nicht, you folk. Some o' you lassies micht gie's a bit sang to cheer's up a wee.

MAGGIE: Weel, fat'll't be, father?

JEANNIE: Oh, I say, Maggie, gie's the "Bonnie Lass o' Fyvie."

JOHN ANDERSON: Ay, that's a fine-gaun ane. (To wife) Div'n ye think that, 'umman? Ye min' ye eest to sing't yersel' lang syne?

A Scots Drama in One Act.

LOVE ON THE FARM

by Highlander.

(Characters)

Effie McLean .... A Widow
Willie Buchan(A Bachelor) ..... A Shephard
Mary McLean (A Milkmaid) ..... Effie's Daughter
Donald Stewart(The Farmer's Son)   A Young Ploughman

Scene: The kitchen of a cottar's house.   Dresser, Table,
Two Chairs and Fireplace.   Time: An early summer
morning.

Effie: (Sitting just finishing her morning cup of tea) Aye, Aye,
folk say farm life is a gey healthy yin; weel, it is;
but a' the same ye hiv tae work gey hard.   At least it
his aye been that wey wi' me ever since I wis ony thing
worth.   But they say that wark's guid for ye, although
ower muckle sune tires ye oot, but I believe in the auld
proverb, "Tae bed wi' the lamb an' up wi' the lark".   And
ever since I lost my man John McLean, Ive aye tried tae
mak' the best o' it; me an' Mary, this bit lassie o'
mine, she's the only ane we ever had an' a' the comfort
I hae left noo, and she's aye dune her best tae keep the
bit hoosie abune oor heids.   But let me see, whit
time is it?(Looking at timepiece) Five o'clock!   By my
certy, it's time Mary wis up.   She wis at a maiden-dance
last nicht and she'll be gey tired this mornin'.   I'll
hae tae wauken her.   Haw Mary!   (Mary does not hear the
first time)   Mary!   Come awa' lassie or the kye will be
cryin' on ye this mornin'.

Mary: Aye mither, I'll be there the noo.

Effie: It's the mornin' that tells.   (Effie working about the house

Mary: Whaur's my shawl mither?

Effie: On the back o' that chair at yer bed.

Mary: Oh aye, I see it noo mither.   (Mary comes into the kitchen
yawning with shawl in hand) Ay aye mither, but I'm a tired
lassie this mornin'.

Effie: Ye will gang tae the dancin' ye see; but I needna say that,
for I wis jist as daft mysel' when I wis like ye.   Haud ye
a guid nicht Mary?

Mary: Oh aye mither, it wis something graund, the best I've been at for a lang time; plenty dancin' and guid singin'.

Effie: Wis Willie Buchan the shepherd there?

Mary: Aye mither, and he sang durin' the nicht.

Effie: Aye, Willie wis a guid Scotch singer in his day. Whit sang did he sing Mary?

Mary: He sang "The Bonnie Lass o' Ballochmyle". Aye, and he came ower and sat beside me efter he wis finished and asked me hoo ye were keepin' mither.

Effie (Smiling) Did he Mary? That wis gey mindfu' o' him. Dae ye want a cup o' tea Mary?

Mary: Oh, no, mither, I'll no hae time; I'll hae tae rin or I'll be gettin' the kick this mornin'. Weel mither, guid mornin' wi' ye.

Effie: Guid mornin' Mary. (Mary goes away) Oh aye, she gangs awa' singin' like a wee lintie. Aweel, Aweel, when the hert is young, everything gangs bricht and cheery. (She comes in and shuts the door).

(Willie Buchan starts to sing outside)

Ca' the yowes tae the Knowes
Ca' them whaur the heather grows
Ca' them whaur the burnie rows
My bonnie dearie.

Effie: Ay! That's Willie Buchan the shepherd singin' tae his sheep and bits o' lambs. Willie and my man John McLean were aye dear cronies. Aye, it wis Willie wha sat his death-bed wi' me nicht and day and seen him breathe his last. Aye, it wis a bad harvest day that for him, the drenchin' he got brocht on the trouble and that wis the end o' it; but ye hae jist tae thole it a'. Aye, jist tae thole it a'. (Effie sits lamenting)

(Willie Buchan enters with stick in hand)

Willie: Weel Effie it's a fine mornin'. An' hoo is the warld usin' ye noo wumman.? Are ye aye keepin' in guid health?

Effie: Weel, I canna complain Willie. Are ye no' sittin' doon a wee while?

Willie: Naw Effie. I'll hae tae gang and be watchin' they sheep. Dae ye ken I've lost ane some wey, and I'm feart tae tell the maister, so I'll be gang Effie and mak' a guid search for it.

Effie: Mary wis tellin' me ye wis at the dance last nicht. Did ye enjoy yersel' Willie?

Willie: I darsay I did; an' I saw Mary there richt enough. Dae ye ken Effie, I think Donal' Stewart the fairmer's son has a bit notion o' Mary. He had her up at very near every dance.

Effie: Oh, Willie, dinna say that! Mary's faur ower young tae hae a laud, an' I dinna think she'll leave her mither for a lang time tae come yet.

Willie: It's hard tae say Effie, but time will tell. Noo I think I'll be gaun an' hae a look roon' for that sheep I lost, but I'LL gie ye a ca' in when I'm passin' this wey and let ye ken if I get it.

Effie: Jist that Willie, an' I'll aye mak' ye welcome for auld times sake.

Willie: Ta-ta the noo then Effie; an' tell Mary I wis askin' for her, will ye?

Effie: I'll dae that Willie. Ta-ta wi' ye. (Willie goes away) Aweel, I think I'll hae a scone or twa bakit tae keep me frae wearyin'. (Knocks heard at door) Wha can this be noo I winder. (Effie opens the door) (Mary enters with arm in sling and Donald Stewart supporting her) What in a' the warld's happened Mary?

Donald: Oh, jist a wee accident Effie. Dae ye ken it wis that new coo we bocht last week. Its a bad yin. Mary wis jist sittin' milkin' quite the thing, when she lit oot an' knocked Mary kickin', milk can an' a'. I dinna think its awfu' bad, altho' she's got a guid lick. Hiv ye ony-thing in the hoose tae rub it wi' Effie? I'm a bit o' a doctor, I yist tae be in the ambulance class ye ken.

Effie: I think I should hae a wee bottle o' embrocation some wey in the hoose. Oh, aye, here it is Donal'. (Effie hands the bottle to Donald from off the dresser)

Donald: Come on Mary, I'll be yer doctor lassie. Let me tak aff that sling. (Takes sling off Mary's arm)

Mary: Oh, Donal' be canny wi' it laddie.

Donald: Oh, I'll be canna Mary. Dae ye ken whit Rabbie Burns said.

Mary: I dinna min' the noo Donal'.

Donald: (Sings) Bonnie wee thing, canny wee thing,
                  Lovely wee thing, wert thou mine.
            (Keeps on dressing Mary's arm while singing)   Noo I think
            that will be an awfu' lump better in a while Mary, an' if
            ye feel onything weel in the efternune, ye'll jist gies a
            ca' up tae the field, ye ken the vin I mean Mary?

Mary: Aye, Donal' , if my mither agrees tae that.

Donald: (Goes over and claps Effie on the shoulder)   Will ye Effie?
            Let her up for a wee while.   The fresh air will dae her a
            lot o' guid.

Effie: Och aye Donal', seein' ye were kind in bringin' her hame
            and baundagin' up her arm sae weel.   An' that wis wan guid
            thing, we didna need tae send for the doctor.

Donald: Aweel Effie, I'll awa, an' jist gie Mary a het cup o' tea
            tae refresh her.   She'll be a'richt in a wee while.
            Ye'll try an' come up Mary?   (Mary nods, smiling)   Ta-ta
            then Mary.

Mary: Ta-ta Donal'.   (Donald goes away)

Effie: He's a fine fellow that Mary.   Is his faither keepin' ony
            -better?

Mary: No mither.   Donal' wis tellin' me he wisna makin' muckle
            o' it.   The hert's a place they canna trifle wi' ye ken.

Effie: Willie Buchan wis sayin' tae me this mornin, that you an'
            Donal' wis gey lovin' like at the dance last nicht.   I
            doot he his a bit notion o' ye Mary, his he no?

Mary: Oh, mither, we could be freenly enough at the dance, an'
            still no nae love between us.   Aye, an' Willie Buchan
            wis in here this mornin'?   He's shairly been awfu' early
            afit efter last nicht's fun.

Effie: Och, weel, Mary, he jist ca'd in a wee while in passin'.
            He wis tellin' me he had lost a sheep an' he gaed awa in
            a hurry tae hae a look for it.

Mary: Aye, mither, but believe me Willie Buchan has some regards
            for you.   Dae ye ken, he wis aye speakin' aboot ye tae me
            at the dance, an' there's nae man wad speak aboot a wumman
            sae muckle if he didna care for her, I ken that muckle
            onywey.

Effie: He wis a dear crony o' yer faither's Mary, an' that's the
            wey we like tae keep up the freenship.

(Willie Buchan is heard singing outside)   Oh, wert thou in the cauld blast, on yonder lea, on yonder lea.

Mary: That's Willie Buchan the noo mither.   Will he be comin' in

Effie: Oh, very likely Mary.   He said he wad ca' in an' let me ke if he got the sheep he lost.

(Knocks heard at the door. Effie goes and opens it)

Ay, jist come awa' in an' sit doon Willie; I've got an invalid since ye ca'd this mornin'. (Mary sitting at fireside)

Willie: (Taking a chair) Oh, its you Mary; an' whit's went wrang wi' ye lassie.

Mary: Oh, jist a kick Willie I got frae frae yon new coo that wis bocht last week.   She's a richt wicket yin.

Effie: Its naething serious Willie; it'll sune get better.   Did ye get the sheep ye lost?

Willie: Aye Effie, I got it wanderin' up at the auld castle yonder. Ye'll ken the place I mean, whaur John and you vist tae walk on the bonnie summer efternunes, an' I often thocht there wisna a brawer couple in the hale country side.

Effie: Ay, Willie, ye're bringin' up happy memories o' the past noo.

Willie: Aye Effie, that's quite true; but keep up yer hert wumman, there micht be happy days in store for ye yet. We never ken whit's in front o' us.

Mary: Weel mither, I think I'll tak a bit walk an' get the fresh air.

Willie: Its a fine day Mary, an' it'll no dae ye a bit o' hairm lassie.   Are ye gaun up tae the farm?

Mary: No Willie, I'm gaun up tae the field whaur Donal' is ploughin'.   I promised I wad gang up an' see him wi' my mither's consent of course.   Weel I'll awa, but I wis gaun tae say (Mary looks shy)

Effie: Whit wis ye gaun tae say Mary?

Mary: Twa's company three's nane. (Mary closes door slowly)

Willie: (Laughing) Dae ye ken Effie, them that's in love are no lik ony ither body. Aye an' believe me, there's love between Mary an' Donal' Stewart as shair as I'm a shepherd.

(6)

Effie: Weel Willie, I'm beginnin' tae think that tae. Donal' cam' doon wi' her when she got the kick frae the coo this mornin', an' he wis gev cheery on it a' the time he wis sortin' her airm.

Willie: I'm tellin' ye, thev're in love Effie. And mind ye, she'll be wrang if she disna wire in for him, for if onything should happen his faither, Donal' wad become heir o' the farm, him bein' the only son, and that wad be something for her. Jist fancv her becomin' Mrs. Stewart and mistress o' the farm as weel. Bv, mind ye its something tae look forrit tae Effie.

Effie: Aye Willie, but I'm lookin' at it in a different wey. What wad I dae if that should happen?

Willie: What wey Effie? Ye're quite young yet, an' ye can aye dae yer ain turn as regards farm wark; or ye micht tak a thocht o' mairyin' again for a' that I ken; that is, if ye got a rale weel dae'in man. Wad ye no?

Effie: Oh Willie, that wad set the country side a-talkin'.

Willie: But ye can please yersel' in that respec' Effie. Never mind what folk say. Dae ye ken Effie, I've ha'en somethin' on my mind tae tell ye this lang time wumman, an' ye're no tae think ony harm o' me when I tell ye what it is.

Effie: Weel, Willie Buchan, dinna be blate an' tell me. It's a gey true sayin' "Open confessions are guid for the soul". So its you tae explain yersel'.

Willie: (Rather Backward) Oh aye, if I only could tak the courage wumman; but I suppose I'll hae tae try. Weel Effie, I'm gettin' tired o' bothy life, an' I've been a lang time a bachelor, so I wad like a bit hame o' my ain an' a cheery, smilin' wife something like yersel' for the rest o' my davs; so I maun tell ye noo Effie, that I love ye wi' a' my hert. Will ye be mine?

Effie: (Shyly) I half jaloused that a' the time Willie, an' ye've been a lang time a faithfu' servant tae the maister, an' if ye look ower a bit hoosie o' yer ain as weel as ye've watched ower yer flock, I maun jist accept yer offer Willie.

Willie: Ay! Effie, an' ye'll be mine! An' we'll be happy the gither for the rest o' oor lives; will we Effie?

Effie: Aye Willie. But hoo can I break the news tae Mary?

Willie: Weel Effie, ye hae a chance tae break the news richt enough. Dae ye ken I didna like tae tell ye, but I heard for truth that Donal' Stewart wis comin' doon tae ask for yer consent tae mairry Mary.

Effie: I doot Willie, this has a' been made up between you and Donal' Stewart, but we'll find oot later on.

(Donald and Mary listening outside door, then come in laughing loudly.

Donald: Oh aye, we heard a' yer conversation. Aye, Wille, an ye've popped the question hae ye. Weel, look here Effie, since Willie has brokeen the ice for me, I'll no be sae backward as him in askin' ye. (Donald looks simple) I've come tae ask for yer consent tae mairry Mary. Say aye Effie, say aye wumman.

Effie: Weel Donal' what can I say but aye, when I hae consented mysel' tae become Willie Buchan's wife; an' I ken fine Donal', you an' Mary will mak a guid match.

Donald: Oh, thank ye Effie, an' I'll try an' mak Mary gey happy. (Donald goes over to Willie and shakes hands) Weel, Willie, ye've managed it gey weel, so we'll jist mak a double event o' it, an' hae the banns cried oot on Sunday first at the auld kirk, an' that'll be a big surprise for a' the folk aroon this country side.

Willie: Jist that then Donal', an' when we get mairret and settled doon side by side, we can baith look back on the happy days when we made love on the Farm.

(Willie Embraces Effie and Donald Embraces Mary)

(CURTAIN)

A NICHT WI' THE DUGS

BY

ROBERT MACLEOD.

THE

GRAND ASSEMBLY

O' THE WHUPPETS.

AT

CENTRAL RECREATION GROUNDS,

COWDENBEATH & LOCHGELLY.

A NICHT WI' THE DUGS
BY
ROBERT MACLEOD

THE

GRAND
ASSEMBLY
O' THE WHUPPETS
AT
CENTRAL RECREATION GROUNDS
COWDENBEATH & LOCHGELLY

A NICHT WI' THE DUGS

Noo, freens, nae doot ye hive seen the tail o' a dug mony a time, altho' ye hivna heard this wee tale o' mine concernin' the duggies that are rinnin' at Cowdenbeath and Lochgelly every Friday and Seterdey. Noo, when I got the idea inta my heid, I just went awa up tae see the judges – Alex. Paterson and Peter Wilson, and I asked them if they didna think the Whuppets needed a wee bit o' sport and enjoyment among themsels, seein' they had dune their best trying tae win a handicap noo and again. So they said tae me, "whit kind o' fun dae ye think we could gie them, Mac?" "Oh," says I, "let us hae a grand assembly wi' them and hae a guid nicht's fun." They said it was a fine idea, so awa we gaed and engaged the biggest hall we could get, seein' we had a great lot o' dugs in the surroondin' district. So we dunnered awa up tae Given & Paton's and got the bills printed, and when they were put in the shop windies a' the folk got a fine laugh at seein' a whuppet's dance coming aff. Weel, the duggies had tae meet in the park first and then march up tae the hall in couples, and when the happy nicht cam roon' yon wis a braw sicht. There wis some o' the brawest dugs and dugess's that ever was slippit by a slipper or ran between wire nettin' tae a rag at the shot o' the pistol.[2] Noo, when the hall door opened there wis an awfu' race tae see wha wad be in first; ye wid just thocht it was a handicap they were at. Weel, efter that, Geordie Taylor, the handicapper, sent the "News Boy" awa doon tae the station tae see if ther kennel freens had arrived frae the East o'Fife. Seein' he had sent the "Telegram" rIcht enough, they cam dressed up in their best, and they taen a "Slow Coach" up tae the hall door. Noo, the grand march started at 10 p.m., and by a' appearance it wis gaun tae be a sure "success," and the "Music" wid be guid as the "Ragtime" band had turned up. Noo, Dickie made an efficient M.C., and when

---

[2] From this point on, MacLeod used the actual names of the dogs to piece together the monologue, presuming that his listeners will recognise the dogs' names while finding amusement in the way they are used to create a storyline.

he blew his whussel for the first reel a' their lugs were cockit, and they flew across tae grab their pairtners. The "Denbeath Lass" and "Wee Crissy" were dressed in "Gat Green" and "All Black" wi "White Tips" on their sleeves. Noo, the "Irish Mall", and the "News Girl" were late in comin', but they said they had been waitin' on "John MacLean" seeing "Lloyd George" wanted "Peace" and "Liberty", "Douglas Haig" cried oot "Carry On" and "Go Right," "That's It." Noo, "Charlie Chaplin" looked "Active" wi' his "Torn Breeks" and "White Socks," so "The Bee" made an "Air Raid" on the back o' his neck and gied him a "Redskin," and he cried oot, "Go On" you "Bummer" you've left a "Wee Tot" on my "Gold Spot" and I'll kick up a "Diadem" you "Cowboy." Efter that "The Fox" had a "Deco" at "Scotch Jimmy" wi his "Glad Eye" tryin' tae steal a bottle o' "No. 10" oot o' "Wee Macgregor's" pooch, so he made a "Flying Scud" at him and gied him a "Nailer" wi his "Iron Clad" on the "Tim Ribs," and said, "I'll learn ye no tae 'Steel Lad': remember "Honesty" is our 'Only Hope'." Noo, when the first interval cam roon there wis some fine singing and dancing which wis "All Good"; the "First Try" was by "Silver Tag" wha sang the "Nameless Lassie" and "Scotland Yet", then the "Artful" "Country Lass," "Wee Bess," wi' a "Greenvale," sang "Prince Charlie" and "Haw Wull" ye no come "Back Again"; "Mick Doolan" sang "I'll take you home again 'Kathleen" "It's a long way to "Tipperary" to "Get Home," but I'll "Be True Girl." "Cheers" went roon the hall when "Fife Jock" sang "Maggie Lauder," wha "Has Been" a wild "Rover". Noo, "Jack" the "Sailor" favoured them wi "Nancy" yer "My Fancy," "I'll be ye ain True Blue.'" The heiland fling was danced by "Wee Meg," "Tit Bit," "Wee Nell," "Peggie Lea," and "Wee Alice." "Neil Gow" played the fiddle, and the "Old One" was fair "Done Up," so they gied him the "Cowslip." The "Gammie Lad" sang "K-K-Katy" go and leave me "Never Mind". Noo pairtners for the waltzin' competition wis cried oot and Dickie, Sharp, and Taylor had an awfu' job chalkin' their heels, and Peter Wilson wis tellin' "Violet" and the "Scots Gray," tae keep on their [tip top ? and

? ?] that she wis nae "Sleeper," ye canna "Catch Me," "Peter," I dinna "Run For Fun," "Wait and See," or ask the "Denbeath Lad," he'll "Be Wise" and "Follow Me." Efter that "Sir Thomas" awarded the prizes tae "Benarty Lad" and "Annie Laurie," and they had tae let in "Fresh Air" as the "May Dew" wis "Lion" on Annie's broo. "Big Wullie" wis sittin' writing "Posey" aboot "Reformation" and "Lucky Meg," so "Bad News" ran roon the hall and asked wha he wis. "Young Tom" cried oot, that's "Little Aggie's" man. Noo, the "Wasp" and "Spider" ran along the "Flash Wire," but fell like a "Snowflake" on a "Primrose Day" on the tap o' "Swallow Drum." "First Down" had his "Hawk Eye" on "Hector" kissing a "Bonny Lass" ca'd "Bunty," and she said she wis as sweet as "Honey Dew" and his loving "Christmas Daisy." Then "King David" began chewing the rag wi' the "Nigger" aboot losing his "Pearl White" collar stud, and blamed the "Sweeper" for it, but "Sniper" shot the "Unknown" "Thief," so he had his "Revenge." "Lady Pet" came in crying I've lost my "Tip It," and they couldna "Stopper" greeting, but efter a "Second Thought" she minded she had lent it tae "Fanny" tae gang hame wi' her "Lad," "Buller," "The Squire." Noo "Wee Andrew" wis kissing "Betty White" in "Her Dream," then an awfu' row got up between "Black Demon" and "Dixie Kid" taking "Nora" intae the refreshment bar, and "Wee Bob" cried tae "Sunny Jim," "Come Quick" and get a "Beer" for I can "Duke II." The ante-room wis crushed fu' and the "White Elephant" fell on the tap o' "Auld Kirsty," "Poor Lass." "Pretty Polly" and "Bonny Jean" were the barmaids. They had to gie her a drink o' tea, then "Meg Dodds" and the auld "China Lass" came running in wi' "Lux" and "Vim" and polished "Jumbo" aff. Noo, "Lazy Boy," wha "Never Won" hame, fell into the fire, and "Red Cap" yelled oot yer "Burnt Lad"; get up and "Zena" will tak' the "Wee Cinders" aff yer back. So when this wis gaun on "Hungry Hill," a fair "Night Hawk," pinched a plate o' sandwiches and went oot the back winda followed by "Davie Haggart," but "Fighting Mac" was on their track and made it "Fatal" for them. Noo, the "Golden Sun" came shining in when "Carolina" dressed in pink was made belle o' the ball, so "Gaity Girl," "Grace Darling," "Poleen," "Coleen," "Lady Lea," and "Nina" shook hands wi' her and wished her long life and happiness and a guid man, so the "lot" o them went doon tae see her awa' on the Kelty car. In the mornin' the East o' Fife lads and lassies got the train at 7 o'clock. They fairly enjoyed themselves, and they wanted a guid rest tae be ready for the bog handicap at Lochgelly on Seterday efternune, and they vowed they wad tell their owners aboot Bobby MacLeod, the chap wha did tell their owners aboot Bobby MacLeod, the chap wha did say he wid like tae hae a nicht wi' the Dugs.

Some Guid Advice

Oh, aye Sandy likit his drap o rale guid Scotch. He didna jist need it tae mak him sleep, no, no, only he couldna gang tae sleep withoot it for fear he didna get ony when did wakin'. Noo freens, I'll gie ye aa guid advice. When ye gaun hame frae the pictures the nicht, if ye find yersel getting heavy ye should eat less and dinna start dosin (like a peerie), but gang tae yer bed an try tae drap ower (no the bed, ye ken) and if ye canna faa asleep, ye maun jist lie waukin.

Guid nicht!

The Last Words o a Miner Poet

Tae the Grave-digger Jimmy Wiseman o Kirk o Beath

If I die and lose my braith
Juist tak me up tae Kirk o Beath
And hand me ower tae Jimmy Wiseman
He'll only think he's got a prize man.

When he sees the hearse coming ower the ben
He'll cry, "Wha is this ye hae the day?"
The driver he'll say, "Dinnae speak aloud,
It's only oor poet, pair Robbie MacLeod.

So open yer gates and let us through
And his last request we'll tell tae you.
Noo Jimmy lay him cannily doon
For ye ken he wis a funny loon.

He wrought beside yer wee son Johnnie,
Wha wis Robbie's faithful cronie.
He made the best o his spare oors
And brocht Robbie mony a bunch o flouers.

But noo pair Mac has slipped awaa
And Johnnie has nae pal ava.
The last words that Bobbie said,
"Tell Jimmy tae be canny wi the spade

And when he's got me in a corner,
Let him play at Johnnie Horner."
Noo Jimmy Wiseman, try yer best
And gie puir Robbie his last request."

Signed by Robert MacLeod, The Miner Poet
79 Union Street,
Cowdenbeath, Fifeshire.
26th. October 1912.

Appendix

Letters to Robert MacLeod

The following pages show some of the letters that Robert MacLeod received in recognition of his talent and generosity. Over the years the pages have been copied and re-copied, but alas we have not been able to find any originals intact. Some papers were found in an old cardboard box, but when Arthur Nevay removed them for copying, it was evident that the edges had been eaten by mice. Though incomplete, they nevertheless show the esteem in which Robert MacLeod was held, and it is reassuring to know that he had the pleasure of receiving such prestigious letters. There is also a sense, however, that there may have been more papers lost than saved from MacLeod's personal archive.

LETTERS FROM
BUCKINGHAM PALACE

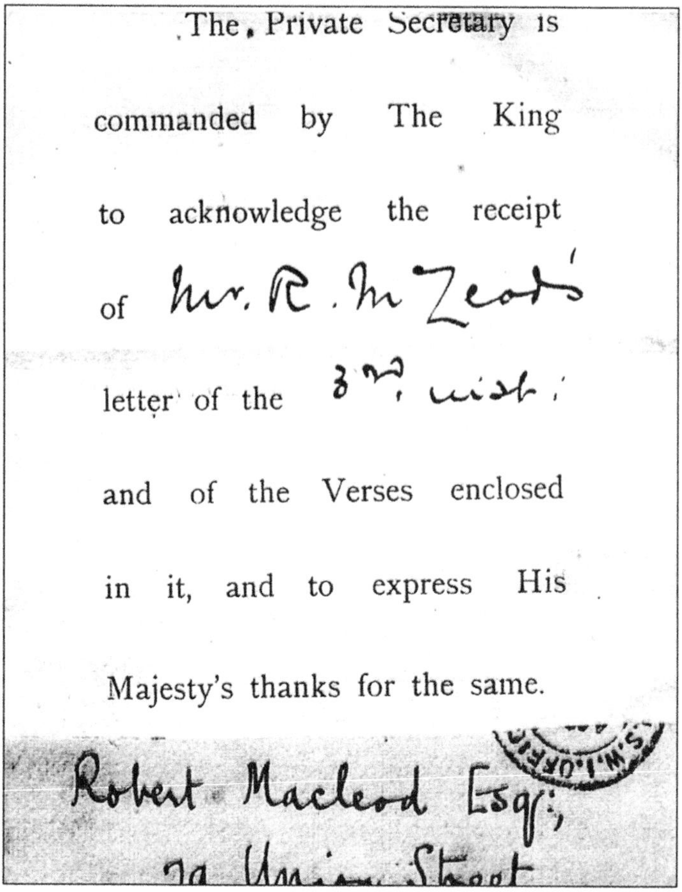

The , Private Secretary is

commanded   by   The   King

to   acknowledge   the   receipt

of *[handwritten: Mr. R. McLeod's]*

letter of the *[handwritten: 3rd, inst.]*

and   of   the   Verses   enclosed

in   it,   and   to   express   His

Majesty's   thanks   for   the   same.

[handwritten: Robert Macleod Esq.,]
[handwritten: 7a Union Street]

Poem *To the Memory of King George V*

BUCKINGHAM PALACE

The Private Secretary

is commanded by Their Majesties

the King and Queen to thank

Mr. Robert Macleod

for *his*   message of sympathy

on the death of Her Majesty

Queen Alexandra.

5. Dec   1925.

Poem To *Tribute to the Memory of the Queen Mother*

ASSISTED IN SENDING CIGARETTES
TO THE TROOPS

W. D. & H. O. Wills

BRANCH OF THE IMPERIAL TOBACCO CO. (OF GREAT BRITAIN AND IRELAND), LTD.

Telegrams:
WILLS, BRISTOL.
CASTLES, CENT, LONDON.
P   CAPSTAN, GLASGOW.
WILLS, BELFAST.

BRISTOL TELEPHONE Nº 63001.

IN REPLY PLEASE QUOTE "DEPT. 22. "

Bedminster
Bristol. 3.

21st March, 1940.

Mr. R. MacLeod,
    169 Union Street,
    Cowdenbeath, Fifes.

Dear Sir,

We have received your letter of the 18th instant
and have read the verses which you enclosed with very much
interest.   We should like to congratulate you on their
excellence, and appreciate the reference made in them to
our brands of cigarettes.   We shall be pleased to make a
gift of 200 "Woodbine" Cigarettes in 10's cartons, which w
would ask you to accept with our compliments for inclusior
in the parcels of comforts which you are sending to the
Troops, and are arranging for the parcel to be forwarded t
you on March 27th.

Yours faithfully,

W. D. & H. O. Wills

Branch   of
The Imperial Tobacco Co. (of Great Britain & Ireland) Limited.

Reply from W. D. & H. O. Wills (Woodbine), when MacLeod sent his
poem *A Jock to his Sweetheart*, requesting cigarettes for the troops.

GENERAL MONTGOMERY

THE WAR OFFICE,
WHITEHALL, S.W.1.

4 October, 1948.

Field Marshal Montgomery has
to thank you for your letter of
shes and for the nice verses which
losed.

Yours *sincerely,*

Major, A.D.C. to the
Chief of the Imperial General Staff.

d, Esq.,
on Street,
ath,
e,
.

After the war, Field Marshall Montgomery wrote to MacLeod thanking him for the poem *The Men of El Alamein*.

SIR ANDREW CARNEGIE

SKIBO CASTLE
DORNOCH,
SUTHER

Abruam 3 1914.

Sir;

Mr Carnegie is much pleased with your
in Dunfermline's Bonnie Glen, and sends His best
to you for it. He is glad to know that the Glen
is so much pleasure to many of the inhabitants of
auld grey toon".

Mr Carnegie hopes you may be interested in the
tion of the enclosed picture, of which he has had
thousand copies distributed.

Respectfully,

[signature]
Secretary

Macleod Esq
on Street,
beath,
re.

17/12/42.   169 Union Street
To Gur J. Flora.   Cowdenbeath
                                         Fife.

Dear.

John just a note tae say,
I hope yer feeling O.K.
("Zam") my son yer old Pal
He's here and whiles on the ball.
He only wishes ye had been
Doon a while frae Aberdeen,
So John auld freen keep up yer chin
The New Year will sune be in,
We'll meet I'm shair and hae a dram
And jist say here's luck tae Zam.

P.S.
John I intended having my
latest poem "The 51st Division"
ready to send you but the
printer has been very busy but
you'll get them when you come on
leave. I send you a copy of
Flora's cinema to let the boys see it
Wishing You the best John.
Your old friend R. MacLeod Miner Poet

Written in 1942 on the inside of a Christmas card and sent to his son's friend. MacLeod had hoped to have his printed version of *Tribute tae the 51st Highland Division*.

Death of Cowdenbeath's Miner Poet

The death occurred on Friday evening of a well known figure in the town in the person of Mr Robert MacLeod, 99 Thistle St., Cowdenbeath. Mr MacLeod was known as the Miner Poet, and he was the author of several hundred poems.

Mr McLeod wrote mainly on subjects pertaining to Cowdenbeath and the mines. He composed verses about all the local mining disasters and the poems were sold in aid of the disaster funds. Several of his other poems he sold for charitable causes. A regular contributor to the "Advertiser", his effusions also included tributes to any successes gained by the Cowdenbeath Football Club and the public bands.

His last contribution fittingly enough was on the Lindsay Pit Disaster. His poems were drawn from a long experience in the mines and a spontaneous appreciation of worthy efforts. Several of his poems also gained Royal acknowledgment.

Obituary of Robert MacLeod, 1959

Poems

POEMS TITLES and *first lines*

Songs

SONG TITLES and *first lines*

Printed in Great Britain
by Amazon